MORE PRAISE

DR. REVENUE'S "PATIENTS" SPEAK OUT

We asked you to create a profile, and you gave us a business-life-changing experience that has propelled us to the top of our industry and brought more rewards than I could possibly list.

—Carey Brazell, President, Meyers Brazell, Inc. Atlanta, GA

It's seldom that I recommend anyone or anything to my clients. John Haskell is one of the few exceptions. Dr. Revenue is the answer to the dilemma of actually getting a marketing plan written and executed. I've seen my clients gain upwards of 30% in sales and profits as a direct result of Dr. Revenue's Clinic. If you're serious about your company's health, get the Rx from Dr. Revenue and call me in the morning.

—J. McCarthy President, Point Advertising, Omaha, NE

Dr. Revenue has worked with me on several of my client engagements and brings hard-hitting, practical sales and marketing solutions designed to enhance sales and profitability. Haskell is a world-class marketer with a wealth of seasoned real-world experience coupled with a "hands-on/make-it-happen" approach to implementation.

—Alfred C. Meyers, Arthur Andersen, Dallas, TX

3

As a result of the clinics, the participating Studios had revenue increases ranging from 8-33% over the previous year. This type of planning obviously has a positive impact on building an effective sales organization!

—Ed Miles, Regional Sales Manager, Techline, Madison, WI

We have worked with John since 1996. He is a wonderful facilitator who has helped us to grow from a four-person company based in a spare bedroom to a regional Management and Information Consulting firm having close to sixty employees that enjoys significant annual revenue growth.

—Mike Moran, President
Affiliated Resource Group, Inc., Dublin, OH

John understands the complexities of selling. He grasped the essence of our company at the very outset.

—George Gananian, President, Star Graphic Arts, Brisbane, CA

You managed to pull together people from six different divisions of our company and show them how to make use of the resources they currently have. Through your efforts, we can now see how we should plan to achieve our sales goals.

—David J. Robertson, Director of Marketing
Dayton Rogers Mfg. Co., Minneapolis, MN

I have completed the Fast Trac II class and turned in my business plan. I am very proud of the plan, and the implementation has already begun. I commend our teacher, Mr. John Haskell (Dr. Revenue®). I was particularly impressed with the way in which he was able to demand that everyone give their best effort without making anybody feel inadequate or like a failure.

—Rev. Philip J. Lance, President
Pueblo Nuevo Enterprises, Inc., Los Angeles, CA

Dr. Revenue has assisted our distribution with numerous professional programs. "Building Business with Effective Business Plans" has become a road map to assured success by our customers. Many have profited through "The Sales Manager's Manual," as developed and taught by Dr. Revenue, using his accumulated years of hands-on experience and professional guidance. A truly comprehensive background complements the results of John Haskell's research, presentation and execution.

—O.B. Kelley, VP Sales, Hunter Douglas, Upper Saddle River, NJ

Dr. Revenue has been instrumental to the growth of Action Paging. After completing a Marketing & Sales Clinic we are "working on our business—not in it!" And the results show.

—David Erkman, President
Action Paging Corporation, Whittier, CA

I met Dr. Revenue at your Inc. High Return Marketing Strategies Conference and hired him to do AVT's first marketing plan. He did a magnificent job!

—Donald O. Dennis, President, AVT, Inc., Littleton, CO

John must have worked all night and the very next morning after our Clinic. I am proud to say we have a Plan for '99 that is complete and already in implementation.

—Jeffrey J. Nestor, President, Techline Studio, Pittsburgh, PA

My experience with Dr. Revenue/John Haskell goes back more than 10 years. His work for the Electronic Representatives Association was the impetus for a long and successful campaign to improve the expertise and management skills of multiple-line manufacturers' representatives in the electronics industry.

—William M. Weiner, President
Weiner Association Management, Chicago, IL

The programs were a slam-dunk, home run, perfect 10! We LOVE Dr. Revenue.

—Diane L. Mitchell, Assistant Director University of Connecticut
School of Business Administration
Family Business Program, Storrs, CT

Dr. Revenue (Haskell) is the man. Period! If you listen to him, your business will grow. Pretty simple. Mine did.

—Jeffrey Turner, President, TSA Design Group
and Ad Out Production, Van Nuys, CA

You accepted a patient whose prognosis was viewed as critical if not terminal. Your quick diagnosis was that major surgery was required to restore this patient to health. I am happy to report that today the outlook is bright for Lykes Meat Group, Inc. Our sales force has stabilized, our volumes are increasing steadily, and most important, our revenue per unit of sales is at levels not seen in years. Your guidance with our marketing plans has received a great response from our customers and company morale is better than ever. As the Chief Surgeon, your work was impeccable and on behalf of the Lykes Meat Group and all of our employees, our sincere gratitude and thanks.

—Todd Hoffman, Vice President Sales and Marketing
Lykes Meat Group, Plant City, FL

The headline says it all, "Aggressive Marketing Saves Company!" Your efforts brought Artwood to the forefront.

—Bruce A. Moss, President, Artwood Desk
Design Manufacturing, Inc., Los Angeles, CA

John, you were the star of the show! Thanks for participating in Inc. Magazine's "High Return Marketing Strategies Conference." Here are a few of the comments people shared with me: "He's a pro; Dr. Revenue took complex problems, broke them down into manageable pieces that I can implement today; the whole conference was great! But John's workshop on "Creating and Launching Your Marketing Plan" made the trip worthwhile!"

—Kevin Gilligan, Conference Producer, Inc., Boston, MA

Dr. Revenue, you were definitely a hit with our members! All indications are they didn't get their fill of your prescriptions.

—Selma Kristel, Director, Business Growth Center
South Metro Denver Chamber of Commerce, Denver, CO

John was able to solidify some suspicions I had about my organization while enacting remedial action in other problems areas he identified. I would not hesitate to recommend John and I plan on utilizing his skills in the future.

—Joshua H. Krengle, President
Acme Window Coverings, Ltd., Willowbrook, IL

What a giant step Weinacht & Associates made by attending your Business Planning Clinic. I am very excited to develop the "Rep of the Future Business Plan."

—Kevin Weinacht, President
Weinacht & Associates, Collinsville, IL

John, as I said during your final sales meeting at Waltco, you are the ultimate professional. The marketing and sales teams have become much more effective.

—Carl E. Rolfe, General Manager
Waltco Engineering Company, Gardena, CA

THE Rx CONCEPT AND INTERACTIVE SERIES

P *rofit Rx* is the first in a series of "*Rx*" books. Each book is written to be used, not just read. Each empowers you, the entrepreneur, with a methodology to prescribe for your company. Entrepreneurs have little time for reading. Action is the most important thing. The *Rx* concept focuses on action to improve every element of your business.

Being Dr. Revenue for many years has led me to see business as a matter of diagnosis and prescriptions. As far back as graduate school, before I was called Dr. Revenue, our professors used this model—look at a business, diagnose the problems, prescribe the solutions.

Very few companies have failed because they generated too much revenue. Therefore, our series starts with a basic prescription for business health—write and implement a Marketing and Sales Plan to increase your sales and profits.

Profit Rx is not just a book. Free interactive support is available to you 24/7 on www.ProfitRx.com. Register on the site to receive free updates and news by email. Each book in the Rx series will have its supporting Web site. We believe *Profit Rx* is the first business book to bring you the benefits of the Internet in this way.

Our *Rx* team is dedicated to helping you achieve business success. The team includes Rick Rhoads, professional business writer and editor; Rick Keating, public relations and promotion professional; Rich Goodnight, professional graphic designer, and the professionals at Executive Excellence Publishing.

Thank you for joining us.

Dr. Revenue®
John S. Haskell

Dr. Revenue® is a registered service mark of John S. Haskell, professional marketing consultant, 1700 Mandeville Canyon Road, Los Angeles, CA 90049-2526, USA.

Profit

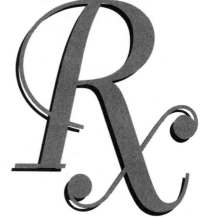

by Dr. Revenue®
a.k.a. John S. Haskell
with Rick Rhoads

> *"My prescription empowers your company to write and implement a Marketing and Sales Plan which increases your profit opportunities immediately."*

Executive
Excellence
Publishing

Profit Rx

For permissions requests, contact the publisher at:
    Executive Excellence Publishing
    1344 East 1120 South
    Provo, UT 84606
    phone: 801-377-4060
    toll free: 800-304-9782
    fax: 801-377-5960
    www.eep.com

For Executive Excellence books, magazines and other products, contact Executive Excellence directly. Call 800-304-9782, fax 801-377-5960, or visit our Web site at www.eep.com.

Printed in the United States

10 9 8 7 6 5 4 3 2 1

ISBN 1-890009-70-9

Library of Congress Catalog Card Number: 99-96834

Cover design by Goodnight and Associates

Printed by Publishers Press

Quantity discount

To order five or more copies of *Profit Rx* for your planning team or business associates, or for use in business courses, call 800-332-0258.

DEDICATION

S ending the first copy of this book to Mom and Dad in Pittsburgh would have been one of the proudest moments of my life. Unfortunately, my Dad, Bud Haskell, died in May, 1996. Mother, Ann Haskell, passed away suddenly July 1, 1999, only a few weeks before the book was completed.

With their love and active support, my parents encouraged me to build my business and enjoy the fruits of success.

Profit Rx is dedicated to their memory, which lives on as the foundation of my work and my life.

ACKNOWLEDGEMENTS

My entrepreneurial career has genetic roots. My two grandfathers and my Dad, Bud Haskell, all built businesses.

Getting out of our family business was a milestone. I was fortunate to work for Milt Slotkin, one of two founding brothers at Abbey Rents. He had "sold out" to Sara Lee (then called Consolidated Foods), but his entrepreneurial roots ran deep. He was a wonderful mentor, building my confidence, reinforcing my self-image and providing a great laboratory for a budding entrepreneur.

Hundreds of clients have bought into the Dr. Revenue ideas of marketing and sales management. I have had the opportunity to formulate plans and help implement them in industries as diverse as sporting goods, furniture, grocery products, moving and storage, printing, computer consulting, and professional services. These businesses provide the examples for *Profit Rx*.

I want to thank every client of The Professional Marketing Group and the Dr. Revenue Marketing & Sales Clinic for trusting me to help their companies move forward in the market and increase profit. The planning system in this book is the direct result of their interaction with me and my teams.

Since 1992, I have had the privilege of teaching an exciting entrepreneurial business training course called Fast Trac™, at the University of Southern California. Many entrepreneurs made commitments of twelve intense weeks to build effective business plans for their companies. The process of working with the Fast Trac students has helped me refine the Dr. Revenue system for marketing and sales planning into a true prescription for profit.

Rick Rhoads has been a skillful collaborator. As an entrepreneur, I want everything "yesterday." Completion of *Profit Rx* has been a long and at times difficult task, accomplished while we were both busy meeting our clients' deadlines. Rick's commitment and knowledge of words and business contributes to the depth and quality of this book.

Finally, Liz Haskell, my psychologist wife. Today she is the president of a cookie company, Country Faire Bakery. We've been together over 30 years. Support has a capital "S" around our house. Life with Dr. Revenue is not always easy. Thank you, Lizzie, for everything.

Dr. Revenue
John S. Haskell

CONTENTS

FOREWORD

By Matthew A. Toledo, President and Publisher,
Los Angeles Business Journal

You are one of a courageous few who have chosen to embark upon the journey of the American Dream; owning your own business. Or you are a key member of the entrepreneurial team. Scores of people dream of entrepreneurial success, but few have the ambition, determination and perseverance to make their dream a reality. I personally have tremendous respect for those men and women who follow their passion and become business owners.

By now, you have established the foundation of your company. You have a product or service, you have employees and you are continually striving to make a name for yourself in the marketplace. You are looking for ways to set yourself apart from your competition. You are looking to build financial strength and evolve as a leader in your field. There are many aspects to growing a business that are crucial elements to the big picture. But probably none so critical as establishing a living, breathing marketing and sales plan.

The Dr. is in . . .

Dr. Revenue has personally written more than 400 marketing and sales plans that have created hundreds of millions of dollars in new opportunity for the companies he has assisted. In Dr. Revenue's

Profit Rx, he shares his painless remedy for creating a marketing and sales plan in just eight weeks.

While most books on business are great anecdotally, *Profit Rx* gives you a chapter-by-chapter blueprint to guide you through the development process so you have a marketing plan in hand at the end of the book.

This book gives you the building blocks and tools to mobilize your team and include them in the procedure of marketing planning. The "working chapters" give you specific goals, guidelines and deadlines for each phase. In addition, www.ProfitRx.com contains agendas for each of the eight meetings, which can be customized and printed for each of the participants. Dr. Revenue provides information and plans that are actionable, presented in a must-do manner.

Constructing a viable marketing and sales plan is an absolute must for any business. This book gives you the benefit of years of experience and success rolled up into an easy to use and execute package. This is a step-by-step remedy for financial health. Take your time, delight in the process and be prepared to achieve your goals of greater profits and longevity. *Profit Rx* is not just a "must read," it's a "must do."

Your plan puts all the tools in place for your sales force to succeed. It eliminates excuses by salespeople.

INTRODUCTION

THE BEST OF TIMES AND THE WORST OF TIMES

Opportunities for business growth have never been greater. Companies or divisions that were small or nonexistent five, ten, or twenty years ago have become industry leaders: Microsoft, Oracle, America Online, Iomega, amazon.com, Southwest Airlines, Wal-Mart, Netscape, Mrs. Fields, Ikea, Saturn, Lexus. For each giant success story, there are hundreds of smaller businesses that have seen their sales and profits rise dramatically in the past decade.

Yet, if you own or work for a startup, the odds are four to one that your business will be out of business before it reaches five years of age. Even if your company is more established, the chance of failure is high. It's hard to come up with an exact number—for example how do you separate a profitable sale of a business from a near-bankruptcy fire sale? Review what's happened to your competitors over the past ten years to get an estimate of the survival rate for your industry. If it's like most industries, failure is epidemic.

As Dickens wrote of the French Revolution, "It was the best of times, it was the worst of times."

Companies that succeed take advantage of rapid change. Companies that fail plod along doing what used to work, until it doesn't. A crisis develops—for example the loss of a big customer—and suddenly comes the realization that our revenues haven't grown enough to see us through.

There's a parallel to maintaining your personal health. Your doctor tells you to exercise regularly and improve your diet. You disregard the advice. After all, nothing has really changed since your 20s, when you could eat anything you wanted. Another few years go by, and you find yourself in an ambulance headed for the ER.

After running several businesses and consulting with over 400 others, I've discovered the business equivalent of proper diet and exercise. It's writing and implementing a marketing and sales plan. Sounds too simple? It is simple—like cutting down on fat. Simple and effective, especially because most of your competitors don't have a plan. In fact, a survey of the Fortune 500 revealed that even among these top companies only 47% have a plan—although they spend an average of 12% of their revenue on marketing and sales. Imagine the wasted time, energy, and money in marketing without a plan. Imagine the tremendous advantages that belong to a company that has a plan.

Without a written marketing and sales plan, you cannot:

- Make the most of your opportunities
- Systematically overcome problems
- Hire and retain the best marketing and sales people
- Initiate action rather than react to external events
- Become or remain the leader in your industry or area
- Position yourself to benefit from change
- Maximize profit

On superficial examination, your business may appear healthy, but it could be heading toward catastrophe.

Perhaps you think your company has a marketing and sales plan; it's just not written down. Baloney. You have ideas that can be the seeds of a plan, but an unwritten plan is an oxymoron. Why?

- Writing is discipline. You separate fact from fantasy; you assign numbers; you expose and eliminate contradictions.

- Your plan includes a marketing calendar and a budget.

- Your plan doesn't change with the daily business winds.

- There is one company plan, not a different plan in the head of each member of your team. Everyone's on the same page instead of doing their own thing.

- Next year you can scientifically review and evaluate the plan, because you will still know what it said.

Not just marketing

Profit Rx is your guide to writing a plan that unites marketing and sales. Companies often develop marketing projects that don't sufficiently take into account the needs and input of salespeople. Given that the whole point of marketing is to meet your customers' needs by selling products and services at a profit, this is absurd. Follow the method in this book and you will have a plan that puts all the tools in place for your sales force to succeed. It eliminates excuses by salespeople.

The bad news

There is only one way to create a written marketing and sales plan. Write it. If there is any bad news, that's it. We all want the goodies that result from the plan, but writing is tough. Thinking is tougher. Finding the time to think and write takes discipline, because you and your staff could spend all day, all night, and weekends putting out fires. But is that the life you aspire to?

The good news

If you and your associates act on the instructions in this book, you'll have a written marketing and sales plan completed within eight weeks from the end of your Launch Meeting. You could do it faster. At a Dr. Revenue Marketing & Sales Clinic, after reviewing a company's situation, I meet with a company's key marketing and sales people for a day, and five days later I submit a written draft of the marketing and sales plan for the coming year. If you stay on the schedule in this book, you're going to meet once a week for no more than four hours, giving you plenty of time to run your business and complete assignments between meetings. On the average, including meetings, each team member should have to put in no more than six hours per week.

This book won't waste your time with general sales and marketing advice. There is plenty of excellent material to fill that need. This book is a tool with one purpose—getting a marketing and sales plan down on paper in eight weeks. Every word in the book, including examples, is there for that reason.

To write your plan, you don't have to be a rocket scientist or a brain surgeon. I'm not. The directions in the book are clear, and are illustrated through examples from real companies. Nobody knows your business better than you and your associates. Combine this knowledge with commitment to creating a plan and the discipline that flows from that commitment, and you will have a plan in eight weeks.

More good news

This book has an agenda for each of the eight meetings you will hold while working on your plan. The agendas are available on www.ProfitRx.com. The project leader can customize them if desired, print them out, and provide each participant with a copy prior to the meeting.

Sample plans and an outline for your marketing and sales plan are also available on the ProfitRx Web site. This saves you time because your plan is already formatted, and it's a psychological boost because no one looks forward to staring at a blank screen. *Dr. Revenue's Marketing & Sales Check-Up* (it's online and on pages 293-299) gets you into the process, and the outline shows you how to put it all together. Your outline does not include prefabricated text because the key opportunities, problems, strategies, and tactics for your company are unique; they cannot be formed with a cookie cutter.

Extra good news

- See results immediately: As you and your associates act on your discoveries and conclusions, marketing and sales can improve even before your plan is completed. Advances may occur after just the first or second meeting. This book presents a proactive, in-the-trenches, do-it-now approach to adding professional planning to your entrepreneurial business.

- A year from now, when you write your second marketing and sales plan, it's going to seem easy, because you'll have the first plan to work from and because you've been through the process. You'll get a better product in less time. And so on, every year.

> **Early returns are 100% favorable**
>
> A fashion accessory company held a pre-clinic meeting to analyze an urgent opportunity. They were exhibiting at five upcoming gift shows. We diagnosed a problem that had prevented the company from taking advantage of previous shows: they exhibited products with no special focus and no compelling incentive for customers to order at the show.
>
> We worked on a new approach, featuring an exciting free-standing display the company had developed. We tightened up the product assortment provided with the display, created a hard-hitting offer for the display plus basic merchandise, added incentive for the company's sales people, and set goals in displays sold and dollars generated for the five shows.

> The results: previous shows had produced an average of $20,000 in sales. Sales at the five shows featuring the display program averaged $40,000, and a new pattern of selling was established.

Based on my experience, your early efforts to put together a plan are likely to result in immediate payoffs. You will analyze aspects of your business that you probably haven't thought of in years, if ever. From the start, you'll identify unnecessary costs and lost revenue opportunities which can be quickly remedied. This will validate the planning process, build momentum to complete the full plan, and increase the revenue stream that can be directed at additional marketing and sales opportunities.

Experience not needed

Many business people know they should have a marketing and sales plan, but delay writing one because they feel they cannot take the time away from more pressing problems and because they feel they don't have the expertise or experience.

Behind this procrastination often looms the vision of a perfect marketing and sales plan—long, researched, footnoted, and suitable for publication in the *Harvard Business Review*. Forget it. Even a poorly worded grammar disaster based on the great deal of knowledge you and your associates already have is better for your company than no plan at all.

Not only does your plan not have to be perfect, it doesn't have to cover everything. In fact, it shouldn't. You may be able to do three or four things well (perhaps just one or two if you are a startup or a one-person show), but not a dozen. In your meetings you'll agree on the three or four highest priority opportunities, put those in the plan, and avoid being distracted by the others. Save the rest in a file for possible use in future plans.

What if it doesn't work?

Closely related to the let's-not-do-it-till-it's-perfect mentality is fear of failure. What if you give your best shot to writing a plan and some of the elements don't work?

So what? You can make a safe bet that few things will work precisely as planned, and some results will be far from expectations. You can't know everything when you write the plan, and even if you could, things change. That's why you evaluate and update your plan quarterly and write a new plan annually. Chapter 10 guides you through the update process.

You can make a safe bet that any plan you develop using the Dr. Revenue guidelines will be far better for your company than no plan at all. Without a plan, there's nothing to evaluate, nothing to update, nothing to improve. Marketing and sales flounder now, later, and until you're out of business.

The wrong decision can be better than paralysis. Particularly when you test tactics before complete implementation, as described in several of the tactics outlined in Chapters 6-8.

Plan leads to new life

The Lykes Meat Group, a $100 million processor of hot-dogs, lunch meat, sausage and hams, was bleeding $1.5 million each month. The Board of the parent company had decided to shut Lykes down unless a convincing crisis-management plan could be developed fast. Dr. Revenue was brought in to lead the marketing and sales component of the turnaround. In two weeks, we documented our goals, strategy, and tactics for the Board. We planned to focus on 20-25 key accounts and get those accounts to re-establish their belief in the Lykes brand. Belief in the brand would allow us to charge supermarkets more for the product, and in turn they could charge consumers more. That would get Lykes out of a pricing box that had developed during five years in which previous management had forgotten that low price is not

29

enough to make a product sell, and that you can't make it up in volume if you are losing pennies on every pound of meat.

We were fortunate to have market research data that showed that Lykes bacon, for example, sold just as well in supermarkets at $2.29 a pound as at $1.99. Consumers saw value even where company management and store buyers had not. Our new marketing plan emphasized getting prices up and supporting those higher prices with innovative merchandising, advertising, and promotion. We developed a group of fanciful cartoon characters, the Lykeables™, that included Betty Bacon, Billy Bologna, and Franky Frank. The Board authorized us to move forward with this plan. It worked. Lykes moved from a loss of $15 million the year before the plan to a significant profit the following year.

Who is this book for?

Entrepreneurial organizations of any size, from one-person start-ups to divisions of large corporations with sales in the hundreds of millions, can successfully apply the ideas and practices described in this book. So can the hundreds of thousands of professionals—lawyers, accountants, bankers, insurance people, brokers, financial planners, money managers, realtors, consultants—who find themselves having to market and sell their services, whether they are sole practitioners or work within a larger entity.

Companies that are growing fast need a marketing and sales plan. Without one, they may find that profits do not grow along with sales. Or they may be so busy trying to keep up with their growth that they lose what got them there, and miss the new opportunities that growth provides.

Profitable companies need a marketing and sales plan to ensure that they are investing to increase their competitive advantage and remain profitable.

Struggling companies need a marketing and sales plan to help turn them around.

Companies whose sales are relatively flat need a marketing and sales plan. Flat doesn't last long. It is a precondition for one of two possible futures: up or down.

Startups need a marketing and sales plan to get off on the right foot.

So much furniture

The Abbey Rents Furniture division of Sara Lee Corporation (Consolidated Foods) had a comprehensive written marketing and sales plan from day one. We started writing the plan six months before we opened our doors, and completed it in time to begin implementation three months in advance. We had even written training manuals, as called for by the plan, a month before opening day.

Preparation was critical. We knew that we were going to be the most expensive rental furniture company in Los Angeles. We also knew that we had the concept for a new kind of rental outlet—one with style, quality, and highly trained sales professionals. Our stores were totally different from the prevailing bargain warehouses, so we made store tours a big part of our marketing and sales plan. We tracked everything—walk-ins, phone-ins—so we knew what effect our advertising had on store traffic. We knew what our closing ratio was each day before we went home.

Our plan focused on generating traffic for a sales force that was hired for killer instinct, then trained to know our products and services and how to sell them. Our goals were clear—close 50% of all walk-ins for $55 a month or more. To reach that average, in addition to furniture, we'd sell extras like posters and other decorative accessories.

At Abbey we knew that without revenue we would be out of business before we had a chance to learn what business we were really in. By working the plan, we developed a strong business, which we then refined. No one had ever rented so much furniture from so little space at such high prices. We succeeded because we planned the marketing, merchandising, advertising, sales promotion, publicity, and sales force management. This early experience proved to me and my associates that solid written planning works.

What is a marketing and sales plan?

I've already discussed why a marketing and sales plan must be in writing.

Chapters 2 through 9 describe the key ingredients of a marketing and sales plan. Briefly, they include the following:

- **Opportunities:** Spell out your opportunities. For example, your present customers like your company and your products or services. Opportunities are generated by competitive advantage. You'll create a Competitive Matrix to evaluate your company against your competitors.

- **Goals:** Based on your real-world opportunities, establish quantifiable, hard-edged goals for the coming 12 to 18 months.

- **Problems:** Identify the major problems that stand in the way of reaching your goals. For example, you're not well known beyond your present customers. Figure out how to use your opportunities to solve your problems.

- **Strategy:** Based on the opportunities, goals, and changes you foresee, what is the relationship between your competencies and your customers? How do you want that relationship to evolve?

- **Tactics:** Define your tactics specifically. Which product or service should we emphasize? What kind of advertising should we do, and where should we do it? Which trade show should we attend, and with what plan? How should we organize our marketing and sales people? Your tactics must drive the company to achieve immediate goals and be compatible with your overall strategy.

- **Marketing Calendar:** Put tactics into a timeline, and assign people to carry them out, with deadlines for completion.

- **Budget:** Create a budget to make sure your plan will be doable and profitable in the real world.

The tactics, marketing calendar, and a well-constructed budget provide the road map for executing your plan. Sales success based on the plan creates a revenue stream that powers the plan and subsequent plans.

The purpose of writing a marketing and sales plan is to implement it. Believe it or not, many plans are written only to collect dust. Chapter 10 helps you ensure that your plan is carried out.

By putting your plan to work, you test it against reality. No marketing and sales plan will ever score 100%. You'll want to update your plan, as well as your sales forecasts, on a quarterly basis or more frequently if developments require. Chapters 11 helps you update your plan.

Chapter 12, "Pulse Report: Numbers to Run Your Business By," is a bonus. It helps you make, implement, and update your plan, and just plain be in control of your company.

It beats the alternative

Writing a marketing and sales plan is like getting older. You may not want to do it, but it beats the alternative. Why is not having a written marketing and sales plan so dangerous?

- You indulge in "reactive marketing." For example, you go to a trade show "because everybody is there." But exactly why are you there?

- Marketing efforts are not directed toward achieving goals. For example, what results do you expect from your advertising?

33

- Without strategic and tactical direction, employees waste time and duplicate effort. The sales process is inefficient and cannot be shaped to maximize profit and revenue.

- Without clear-cut, measurable goals you cannot tell if you are succeeding. Therefore, you would have no basis upon which to adjust your plan—if you had a plan. For example, a direct mail package gets a 1.6% response. How do you swiftly decide whether to send it to additional zip codes?

- Inefficient use is made of marketing and sales funds, including the creation of "black holes." In the physical universe, black holes absorb all energy that comes near them, and emit none. In the marketing universe, money goes into a black hole and nothing comes out. No matter how good its product or service or how dedicated its people, no business can squander revenue and survive.

Competitive advantages of a marketing and sales plan

- Writing a marketing plan forces you to analyze your competitive environment (create a Competitive Matrix); analyze your customers' buying motivation; make sales forecasts; and create or refine a sales system. Do just these four things and you are likely to be ahead of 80% of your competition.

- The process requires examining opportunities, defining measurable goals, and openly confronting obstacles. You resolve critical problems rather than allowing them to linger and worsen.

- By involving frontline sales people, your sales forecasts, sales systems, and goals can be based in reality.

• When management and staff all see the same plan, they can take ownership of it and understand their role in it. You have created a context in which morale can increase and performance can improve—and be measured.

• There is nothing like a map to increase confidence. The plan shows you and your investors the road to realizing company goals.

• The plan creates confidence about your success among your suppliers and distributing partners. Their support is vital to your success.

• Your tactics for the next 12-18 months will increase sales and profits for that period, and will also conform to your long-term strategy for positioning your organization.

Let's write your plan

Now that you have read this far, you are probably convinced that writing a marketing and sales plan is a vital ingredient of success. As convinced as you may be now, it is going through the process and seeing the results that will make you and your associates true believers. This book will guide you through each step of writing your plan, from beginning to end. Additional help from our Internet support line is a click away at www.ProfitRx.com.

Please begin the process of writing your company's marketing and sales plan by filling out *Dr. Revenue's Marketing & Sales Check-Up*. It's on pages 295-301, but it's even easier to use on www.ProfitRx.com.

Write Your Marketing and Sales Plan

Preparation and Agendas for the 8 Planning Meetings and for Update Meetings

Interactive support

All preparations and agendas are posted on www.ProfitRx.com. You can download them and customize them for your company's meetings.

If you have questions or suggestions on how to structure your meetings, or about any other part of the planning process, send email to me at drrevenue@ProfitRx.com.

Heads-up to team leaders and members

Before Meeting 1, set in motion a process that will produce the sales forecasts—from frontline salespeople—that you will need for Meeting 3. Do not wait until after the first two meetings. It will be too late. *Profit Rx,* Chapter 3, pages 120-128, explains why you need sales forecasts and describes how to get them.

If possible, decide before Meeting 1 who is going to write the plan. This is critical: the team is going to make lots of great decisions, but they will be lost unless promptly committed to words on paper. See "Decide who will actually write the plan," *Profit Rx,* page 76.

Create a procedure to write and distribute a draft of the conclusions from each meeting to all team members before the subsequent meeting.

Maximize return on the time you invest in meetings

The outcome of a meeting is determined 90% by the preparation of the participants. Each of the "Preparation" sections below is designed to be used as a detailed checklist, so that you go into every meeting fully prepared to achieve maximum results.

Each of the agendas will help keep you on track during the meetings.

At all your meetings, use Dr. Revenue's Rules of Order to accomplish a lot in a short time.

Dr. Revenue's Rules of Order

1. Stay focused on the written agenda. Alert each other when digressions or tangential discussions prevent progress.

2. Don't get caught up for too long on any one point; first survey the territory.

3. Don't be a lawyer. Pursue truth, not victory.

4. If you tend to talk too much, cut back and encourage others to give their opinions.

5. If you tend to remain silent, think about one point you feel strongly about, and speak out about it.

6. Keeping the meeting on track is everyone's responsibility, but it is especially the moderator or chairperson's responsibility.

Meeting 1: Launch your plan

Preparation for Meeting 1

All team members

Recommended Read *Profit Rx* cover to cover, so that you have an overview of the entire planning process, then review the Introduction and Chapter 1.

Jump start In *Profit Rx,* read the Introduction and Chapter 1.

Complete *Dr. Revenue's Marketing & Sales Check-Up.* (Copy the *Check-Up* from the book or download it from www.ProfitRx.com.)

No later than 48 hours before the meeting Give a copy of the "Results" section, on the last page of your Check-Up, to your Team leader or team administrator. Include your 3 ideas for improving your marketing and sales programs immediately. In the interest of encouraging forthrightness, we suggest that the "Results" and "Improvement Ideas" be submitted anonymously.

Make notes for the meeting on who you believe your main competitors are.

Team leader or team administrator

Average the scores on the "Results" section of the Check-Up and enter them on a fresh copy of the "Results" page. Make copies for all team members.

List all the ideas team members have submitted for immediate marketing and sales improvements. Group similar ideas, or ideas about the same program. Indicate with hash marks when more than one team member has submitted the same idea. Make a copy of the list for each team member.

Bring two blown-up display copies of a blank competitive matrix form (basically just the grid and your company's name). You can use the form on page 302 of *Profit Rx,* or from ProfitRx.com. Have two 8.5x11 copies for each team member to make notes on. (Two because you may decide to create direct and indirect competitive matrixes.) If you intend to do things digitally, have a projection computer in place and tested, with the competitive matrix document open on screen.

Agenda for Meeting 1

Time figures after each item are guidelines. If a segment of the meeting takes less time, great. If it's taking more time but you are on a roll, continue, and try to buy the time back from another item.

1. Discuss why you are writing a marketing and sales plan, and what it can do for your company. Even if each team member has already been involved in such a discussion, it's important to go over it with everybody together. Seek each team member's input on the most useful result of writing the plan, and on how the plan will help the team member perform his or her job. On reviewing the Introduction, we came up with this way of summarizing the advantages of a plan: "A written marketing and sales plan is your biggest competitive advantage, because it allows you to get maximum benefit from all your other competitive advantages." [15-30 minutes]

2. If it hasn't been determined already, decide how your plan will actually be written. See *Profit Rx,* page 76. [5-15 minutes]

3. Distribute and discuss the averaged results section of *Dr. Revenue's Marketing & Sales Check-Up.* What does it tell you about your company's strengths and weaknesses, and about what you need to focus on in writing the plan? Also go over the suggestions for immediately improving marketing and sales, especially those that were suggested independently by several team members. Can anything be done right away, without waiting for the plan to be completed? If so, decide how it will be implemented and who will implement it. Avoid going into so much detail that the rest of the agenda is derailed. Detail can be worked out later by those responsible. [30-60 minutes]

Break [15 minutes]

4. Post the blank competitive matrix. Decide by consensus on who your main competitors are, what the parameters of comparison should be, and how the numerical grading system will work for each parameter. Enter the names of the competitors and the parameters, and make notes about how the grading system works. (See page 84 for an example.) Make copies: each team member should leave the meeting with a customized competitive matrix to fill out. Decide whether you need a second competitive matrix for indirect competition, and, if so, complete it. Usually there is no need to name indirect competitors; just develop parameters that compare your product or service with all indirect competitors of a similar type. [60-90 minutes]

5. If you haven't done it already, schedule the next seven meetings. If that's not possible, schedule the next three. [5-10 minutes]

6. Review expectations: attend all meetings on time; no early departures; complete all actions on time; be honest about concerns (no "yes" people needed) and be open to others' ideas (no know-it-alls needed). [5-10 minutes]

7. Finally, the most burdensome item on the agenda. Discuss and agree on the reward for the team when the project is completed and the plan is written. A pizza party? A day off? An outing with family at the ball park? And how will the other people in your company be involved? [15 minutes]

8. Review preparation for the next meeting. Make assignments. [5-10 minutes]

If you follow the allotted times on the agenda, the length of this meeting, including the break, ranges from 2-1/2 hours to 4 hours 15 minutes.

Meeting 2: Discover opportunities

Preparation for Meeting 2

All team members

Write down your company's largest sales areas (by product, customer, geography—whatever is relevant). Add areas that are small now but you believe have large growth potential. Refer to these notes periodically to help keep you focused on major opportunities

Review Section III (Definitions of Opportunities) in *Dr. Revenue's Marketing & Sales Check-Up.*

Read or review *Profit Rx* Chapter 2 to stimulate your thinking about where to find opportunities.

Complete your competitive matrix by assigning numerical grades. Also complete the indirect competitive matrix if the team decided to use one. Competitive matrixes can be kept anonymous.

Come to the meeting prepared to suggest at least five marketing and sales opportunities open to your company, and at least two non-sales ("soft") opportunities. (See *Profit Rx,* pages 94-107, 128-131).

No later than 48 hours before the meeting Hand in copies of your competitive matrix(es) to the team leader or team administrator.

Reminder for Meeting 3 The process of preparing sales forecasts for the third meeting should already be underway; it should be followed up on or started immediately. See Chapter 3, pages 120-128.

Team leader or team administrator

Average the ratings on the competitive matrixes. Prepare a master (consensus) competitive matrix with these averaged ratings, and distribute them at or (if possible) before the meeting, to help direct the planning team toward the best opportunities.

Agenda for Meeting 2

1. Make sure everyone agrees on what your largest sales areas currently are. [5–10 minutes]

2. Distribute and review the Master Competitive Matrix(es); revise if necessary. [10–20 minutes]

3. Based on your largest and/or potentially largest sales areas and the Master Competitive Matrix(es), brainstorm to create a list of opportunities: at least 5 for a startup, 10-20 for an established company. Include non-sales opportunities. Be sure that each team member speaks about the opportunities he or she brought to the meeting. Put all opportunities on a white board or flipchart, grouped by product or in some other relevant way. Another approach: Team members can submit opportunities on 3x5 Post-it® notes, which can be displayed in appropriate groupings. Or, if you prefer things electronic, use a projection computer and later distribute the file to team members via your network. Just list the opportunities; don't stop to critique them. [1 to 1.5 hours]

Break [15 minutes]

4. Use consensus to agree on the top five opportunities. Rate their ballpark revenue potential over a logical period, such as three years. One way to reach preliminary consensus before discussion: each team member privately lists the three opportunities he or she thinks will generate the most revenue 1-to-3 years out, and submits them to the team leader or administrator. The leader or administrator then compiles and distributes the Top-10 list, marking the 5 that received the most votes, and posts the top 5 opportunities. (The team should keep a record of opportunities that did not make the top 10.) Decide on the opportunities you intend to pursue in the coming year. [30 minutes–1 hour]

5. Review preparation for the next meeting. Make assignments. [10–20 minutes]

Based on the allotted times, the length of this meeting, including the break, is from 2 hours 10 minutes to 3 hours 45 minutes.

Meeting 3: Set goals

Preparation for Meeting 3

All team members

Read or review *Profit Rx* Chapter 3, to stimulate your thinking about setting goals and sales forecasting.

If any information related to your largest sales areas, your Competitive Matrix(es), or the opportunities you just developed is missing, specific team members should be assigned to gather that information and get it to the Team Leader or Administrator within three working days, so it can be distributed to the team before the next meeting.

Review Section IV of *Dr. Revenue's Marketing & Sales Check-Up*, on Sales Goals/Forecasting. Obtain the forecasts mentioned in that Section, with the participation of the salespeople responsible. (This assignment was given before Meeting 1; this is a checkup to make sure forecasts are arriving on schedule.)

Write down what you believe is a reasonable goal for each opportunity (including "soft" opportunities) that the company intends to pursue. Be prepared to explain your thinking at the meeting.

Team leader or team administrator

Guarantee that sales forecasts are received no later than 3 days before Meeting 3, and immediately distribute them to all team members.

Agenda for Meeting 3

1. Review the opportunities you selected last week. (Reconsider them if information that was unavailable or not discussed requires it.) Set goals related to those opportunities. Use relevant forecasts obtained from salespeople. The reality-based goals either confirm the relative value of the opportunities or provide reasons for moving to opportunities you held in reserve. Sometimes it's wise to hold off on definite changes until potential problems are evaluated at next week's meeting. [30-60 minutes]

2. Place these goals in the context of sales goals for the entire company (or division). Again, use relevant sales forecasts. [30 -60 minutes]

Break [15 minutes]

3. Set goals for your non-sales opportunities. [40-60 minutes]

Note: If possible, team members should leave the meeting with a copy of the goals developed in items 1, 2, and 3 above. Otherwise, the team leader or administrator should deliver a copy of the goals to each team member within 24 hours after the meeting.

4. Review preparation for the next meeting. Make assignments. [10 minutes]

Based on the allotted times, the length of this meeting, including the break, is from 1 hour 55 minutes to 3 hours 25 minutes. That gives you at least 35 minutes in reserve to use where needed.

Meeting 4: Problems

Preparation for Meeting 4

All team members

Read or review *Profit Rx* Chapter 4, to stimulate your thinking about identifying problems (not enough honesty, responsibility, money, time, human resources, information).

Review Section V of *Dr. Revenue's Marketing & Sales Check-Up.*

Come to Meeting 4 prepared to discuss at least two problems you anticipate when attacking opportunities. You are not required to have solutions. For next week, at least, it will not be a sin to have a problem without a solution. You will go to hell, however, if you come to the meeting without problems. (You'll develop solutions in Meetings 6 and 7, on tactics.)

Agenda for Meeting 4

1. Review the goals you set last week. Reconsider them if information that was unavailable or not discussed requires it. [10-30 minutes]

2. Compile a list of problems that could prevent you from reaching each of your goals, including your non-sales-related goals. Be sure the problems are specific to your goals, not generalized gripes. For now, don't worry about solutions. If it appears that a problem is so severe that it precludes one of the opportunities you selected, consider replacing that opportunity with another from your list or focusing more intensely on the remaining opportunities. Don't make the final decision to abandon an opportunity until Meeting 6 or 7: time may help you find a solution. [60-150 minutes]

Break [15 minutes, during previous agenda item]

3. Review preparation for the next meeting. Make assignments. [10 minutes]

Based on the allotted times, the length of this meeting, including the break, is from 1 hour 35 minutes to 2 hours 25 minutes.

Meeting 5: Strategy

Preparation for Meeting 5

All teams members

Read or review *Profit Rx* Chapter 5 to stimulate your thinking about strategy and why you could decide to skip this step this year.

Prepare a written "concept statement" for your business (see pages 168-175). Write a draft of an actual one or two paragraph concept statement, not notes or ideas for a concept statement. Your draft should be your own; consensus will be achieved at the meeting.

No later than 48 hours before Meeting 5 Deliver your draft concept statement to the Team Leader or Administrator.

Review other draft concept statements you should receive 24 hours before the meeting, and make notes of your reactions.

Team leader or team administrator

If necessary, follow up to get draft concept statements.

Copy and distribute draft concept statements to all team members no later than 24 hours before Meeting 5.

Agenda for Meeting 5

1. All team members should have already reviewed each draft concept statement. If not, devote the first portion of the meeting to individually reading the drafts and making notes. Even if everybody has done it, allow time for team members to review their notes. [10-25 minutes]

2. Discuss the drafts, and develop a consensus concept statement. Usually, you can select one draft as the starting point, and improve it by deletions, modifications, and additions of elements from other drafts. After the content issues are decided, you may want to assign a team member to edit the concept statement after the meeting. [45-90 minutes]

Break [15 minutes]

3. Develop any additional strategy you require beyond the concept statement. This could relate to development of a new product or division, a new strategic alliance, a new market segment. [5 minutes to decide you don't need to; up to 120 minutes if you do]

4. Review preparation for the next meeting. Make assignments. [10 minutes]

Based on the allotted times, the length of this meeting, including the break, is from 1 hour 25 minutes to 4 hours 10 minutes.

Heads-up to team leaders and members

In Meeting 8, you will be putting together a marketing and sales budget. Where outside vendors are involved, you'll need estimates that reflect your tactics in detail, not figures based on vaguely defined projects that generally end up way off. (See pages 248-249.) Therefore try to work out the details as early as possible after developing a tactic, in conjunction with your outside vendors where appropriate, so that you can come to Meeting 8 with reality-based data. If complex projects or multiple vendors are involved, schedule a 2-week interval between Meeting 7 and Meeting 8.

If you have time in Meeting 6 or 7, use it to plan how to market and sell your completed plan inside your company (See pages 259-261). Otherwise, hold a special short meeting for this purpose. Assign a team member to present a plan for discussion.

Meeting 6: Develop tactics

Preparation for Meeting 6

All team members

Review the lists of opportunities, goals, and problems from Meetings 2, 3, and 4. Make notes of possible more useful ways of viewing the problems.

Review Sections VI and VII of *Dr. Revenue's Marketing & Sales Check-Up.*

Read *Profit Rx* Chapters 6, 7, and 8 to help stimulate your thinking about tactics. Tactics are solutions to problems.

Come to Meeting 6 prepared to suggest at least one tactic to take advantage of each opportunity (or achieve each goal or overcome each problem, depending on which way of looking at it you find most useful). This will be a brainstorming session. Therefore it is not necessary at this point (and it could be a waste of time) to carefully research tactics or nail down details. Do this for the tactics you like best *after* Meeting 6.

Several days after Meeting 5, review the consensus concept statement developed at that meeting. Note any suggestions for improvement. Make sure that the tactics you propose are compatible with the concept statement and any other strategy developed at Meeting 5.

Team leader or team administrator

Circulate a clean, double-spaced draft of the consensus concept statement developed at Meeting 5 to all team members as soon as it is available, no later than 48 hours before Meeting 6.

If other strategy has been written, circulate that as well.

Agenda for Meeting 6

1. Review the consensus concept statement and make any necessary modifications. [5–30 minutes].

2. Brainstorm on possible tactics to take advantage of your opportunities, reach your goals, solve your problems, and carry out your strategy. Start with free and almost-free tactics, then go on to worth-it tactics. If a worth-it tactic comes up out of order, be flexible. The team member proposing a tactic can briefly (a minute or two) explain why it's a winner. Don't stop to critique the tactics; just keep them flowing. Put them up on a flip chart or white board, or use 3x5 Post-it® notes, a projection computer...whatever methodology you are using. Group together tactics that are similar or that address the same problem. [2–3 hours, including a 15-minute break]

3. If possible, arrange for everybody to leave the meeting with a copy of all the proposed tactics. [10 minutes]

4. Review preparation for the next meeting. Make assignments. [10 minutes]

Based on the allotted times, the length of this meeting, including the break, is from 2 hours 25 minutes to 3 hours 40 minutes.

Meeting 7: Refine tactics

Preparation for Meeting 7

Team leader or team administrator

If they did not leave Meeting 6 with a list of all proposed tactics, circulate a copy of the list to all team members as soon as possible—within 24 hours.

Prepare a poster-size display of all the tactics (or the equivalent) for Meeting 7.

All teams members

Review the tactics proposed at Meeting 6. Select the two (or more) that you believe are most likely to produce the greatest return. Come to Meeting 7 prepared to explain the advantages of the tactics you've selected (including cost effectiveness), and with a plan for carrying them out, including deadlines and who should be responsible. Start your review right after Meeting 6, so that once you select your preferred tactics you have time to research the details, including costs.

Agenda for Meeting 7

1. Display the poster-size list of all tactics, or the equivalent. Take a quick survey to see if there's a convergence of opinion on which tactics are the best. Label those. [5–10 minutes]

2. If a convergence was discovered in Item 1, start out with those tactics. In any case, hear from everybody on what tactics they think are best and why, why they are cost effective, and how they would be implemented, including who would be responsible. [90–180 minutes, including a 15-minute break]

3. If it hasn't already happened during Item 2, decide on which tactics to pursue and who is responsible for their implementation [0-60 minutes]

4. Review preparation for the next meeting. Make assignments. [10 minutes]

Based on the allotted times, the length of this meeting, including the break, is from 1 hour 45 minutes to 4 hours 20 minutes.

Meeting 8: Make a calendar and budget

Preparation for Meeting 8

Team leader or team administrator

Make sure that the responsibility for each tactic that will be part of your plan is assigned to a team member. Even if the team member will not be the person in charge of the activity day-to-day, he or she must submit calendar and budget information about the tactic. If you are working digitally, make sure that everyone understands the agreed upon protocols and conventions, so that you can seamlessly merge the data.

Follow up if necessary to receive calendars and budgets 48 hours before the meeting, and distribute them to team members.

Guarantee that necessary materials are at Meeting 8:

• Extra index cards

• A large format calendar for the period of the plan, and/or

• Appropriate calendar or project management software, set-up and ready for use to create the master marketing and sales calendar

• A ledger or software for the master marketing and sales budget

All team members

Prepare calendar (calendar format or list of dates, whatever the team has agreed on) and budget for each tactic you are responsible for. Submit to team leader or project administrator no later than 48 hours before meeting, for immediate distribution to all team members.

Calendar See the example on pages 239-241. Work backwards from your tactic's completion date, and assign a date to each step of the process. Build in cushions to allow time for overcoming problems.

Submit the calendar to the Team leader or team administrator no later than 48 hours before Meeting 8. If the team plans to assemble the master calendar from index cards, prepare a separate index card for each date. Enter the date, the name of the tactic, and the step on the card, and bring the cards to the meeting in chronological order, from earliest to latest. (If you are working digitally, do the equivalent.)

Budget Prepare a detailed budget for your tactic which includes all related expenses. Make sure that outside vendors are quoting on the actual work they will be doing, not some vaguely defined approximation that could result in the estimate being off by an unacceptable margin. (See pages 248-249.) Submit the budget in the agreed upon form to the team leader or team administrator no later than 48 hours before Meeting 8.

Review the other calendars and budgets you receive, and make notes of any questions or comments about them you want to raise at the meeting.

Agenda for Meeting 8

1. Each team member responsible for a tactic raises any questions or issues about that tactic's calendar which requires input from the team. Team members should already have read the calendar, and have copies in front of them, so it should not be necessary to go through every step in detail. The team discusses anything that needs to be resolved, then moves on to the next tactic. [20-45 minutes]

2. Construct the master calendar, based on the individual calendars as amended (if they were) during the above discussion. One way to do this is to merge all the index cards into chronological order, then go through and see if any conflicts are revealed. Or to merge the electronic files. It's important to visualize all the schedules together to find conflicts. Once any conflicts are resolved, enter all the data onto the master calendar, using different colors or some other form of coding for each tactic. If the mechanical aspects of this task will absorb too much time, assign it to a team member and/or staff to complete after the meeting. [30-60 minutes]

Break [15 minutes]

3. Go through a similar review process for each tactic's budget. [20-45 minutes]

4. Examine the marketing and sales budget as a whole. Is money allocated where it will produce the most return? Are expenditures feasible, or must some tactics be modified or postponed? Make any necessary adjustments; record resulting master budget. [30-90 minutes]

. 5. Review method for the following (see pages 258-261):

> Completing first draft of your plan
> Completing final draft of your plan
> Distributing the plan
> Celebrating the completion of the plan and launching its implementation [15 minutes]

When you reach the end of the eighth meeting your plan is completed except for the final writing. You have reached a major milestone in your company's development. This might be a great time for the team to go out and have a drink, or whatever the equivalent is in your corporate culture.

Based on the allotted times, the length of this meeting, including the break, is from 2 hour 10 minutes to 4 hours 30 minutes.

Quarterly meetings to update your plan

Chapter 9 is about when, why, and how to update your plan. You should review your plan at least quarterly—more often, such as every month or six weeks, if your company is in a quickly changing environment. Of course if developments require it you should review and modify your plan without waiting for the scheduled meeting.

Preparation for Update Meetings

Team leader or team administrator

One month before the meeting: Take whatever steps are necessary to get sales forecast updates from salespeople in time to distribute them three days before the meeting.

The update meeting should be on the calendars of all team members. Nevertheless, remind everybody two weeks in advance, and possibly again one week in advance. Include the meeting preparation and agenda in your reminder.

All teams members

Reread the plan. Make notes about the results so far and how they might suggest improvements over the next 3-6 months. Based on your first quarter, do the tactics you are carrying out make sense or do they need to be changed, or even scrapped in favor of different ones? Also consider whether any external changes in the marketplace require tactical adjustments. When the updated sales forecasts arrive, review them from the same point of view.

Dig into the details. For example, your overall numbers may be right on target, but sales to one key customer (or territory, product line, etc.) may be way off, while other sales are higher than expected. What can the team learn from this that will improve the plan in the upcoming quarters?

Go over the budget, especially those parts of it that you are responsible for. How do the actual expenses compare to the projected expenses? Is modification necessary because actual expenses have been higher or lower than expected?

Review the calendar, especially those projects for which you are responsible. Are the steps for each tactic being completed on schedule? Are modifications necessary?

Think about this question: Is marketing serving sales? Is the plan helping to eliminate excuses by sales people? [See page 25.]

Agenda for Update Meetings

1. Use your experience from the eight meetings you've been through to help you come up with the most efficient Update agenda. One logical approach is to simply number the preparation items above 1 through 5 and discuss them in that order, allotting as much time to each as required.

2. Final agenda item: How can we start the next quarter off with a bang? Should we broadcast the results of the quarter now ending and remind everyone that we are working this plan?

Often there is doubt about whether or not to stick with a tactic, modify it, or abandon it. Please see page 278 on that question.

This meeting should take from 2 hours to 4 hours, depending on the extent to which you decide to modify your plan.

Study your competition in relation to yourself. This gives focus and purpose to your information gathering, and leads directly to opportunities for your company.

CHAPTER 1

LAUNCH YOUR PLAN

Congratulations on taking the first step toward writing a marketing and sales plan. You've started reading this book, and hopefully you have stimulated your thinking about your company's strengths, weaknesses, and opportunities by completing *Dr. Revenue's Marketing & Sales Check-Up,* as I suggested at the end of the Introduction.

Now what? We recommend the following approach:

1. Read this book
2. Decide who should be on the planning team
3. Decide who should lead the team, and whether to have a project administrator
4. Decide whether to have an outside facilitator
5. Decide who will actually write the plan
6. Explain the project to the team members
7. Provide each team member with a copy of *Profit Rx*
8. Assign responsibilities for the first meeting, and alert team members of upcoming assignments that require lead time
9. Decide where to meet
10. Decide when to meet

The details

This section is devoted to the details of how to build your planning team and launch your planning process. It may not be as thrilling as reading about how to compare yourself to your competition, which comes right afterward, but I promised you that this book would guide you every step of the way in creating a written marketing and sales plan, and I intend to keep that promise. So, without apologies, here are the details of our method for getting started.

1. Read the book

As with any project, it's good to see the big picture before getting caught up in the details. That way you won't arrive at week seven in the planning process and say, "Oh, if I'd known that, I would have acted earlier." For example, when you discuss strategy, in Meeting 5, you may want information about trends in your industry or in your marketplace. Knowing that, you can take action now to make that information available when it's needed.

Reading the whole book will also give you a better handle on whom to include in your planning team.

However, if reading the whole book is likely to take you months or more unless you get others involved, consider moving directly to the next step and reading along with the other members of the team. Our approach to planning is that "Do it now" beats "Do it perfectly (much) later." Sometimes it's obvious, as in the following example, that your survival is at stake, but having a plan sooner rather than later is always a plus.

Plan now, not later

At Waltco Manufacturing IBM not only provided 95% of all revenue, but the parts that Waltco was making for IBM were for machines that were scheduled to be discontinued within 18 months. At that point backlogs and incoming orders would quickly approach $0.00 after resting at a comfortable and profitable $18 million for many years.

The problem was that all attention went to IBM and Waltco just did not seem to be able to find other business that would become substantial enough quickly enough. Without a plan, everyone's attention was focused on meeting current demand and putting out fires, even though they realized they were on a fatal course.

The marketing and sales plan focused on changing the balance. The results: IBM continued buying from Waltco, which sold them on their ability to make parts for other machines. The new "non-IBM sales force" brought Digital, Hewlett Packard, and several other business on board. Changing habits built up over many years took rigid discipline, firing two sales people, and a hard-fought battle for a new compensation and incentive system for sale personnel bringing in non-IBM business. We made these changes in time to avert the impending disaster. We were lucky at times, but it was a clear example of "making your own luck" through hard, smart work.

2. Decide who should be on the planning team

The key leaders of marketing and sales should be on the team. If an owner, president, or CEO is—or should be—heavily involved in marketing or sales, that individual should be a team member. One or more frontline salespeople can add great input and reality checks. Membership on the team can also be a means of developing staff members who may have an important role in your company's future. If you have a leader of R&D, he or she could be a great addition to the team.

What about people who by their position alone could or could not be on the planning team, for example, the head of credit or the head of customer service? Your judgement call should be based on many factors, including their personalities and other responsibilities. My general advice is to include them if you think they could make a positive contribution and would not make the team too large. If you don't think someone needs to be on the team, but they want to participate and would be offended if not selected, consider including them to avoid creating a negative situation. A rejected player may oppose or even subvert any marketing and sales plan the team creates, simply because they weren't invited.

If your company does not operate with open financial statements, take that into account in building the team. To function meaningfully, team members should have access (at a minimum) to data concerning sales, gross profit and margin, and cost of goods for all products and services.

Managers are sometimes reluctant to involve salespeople in meetings of this nature. They've experienced salespeople sitting back with arms folded, exuding cynicism without saying a word. And they've experienced the other side of the coin—endless unconstructive complaints. Why do many of the best salespeople project the attitude that they cannot learn anything from the sales manager, the president, or even the world's greatest expert in the industry? The life of a salesperson is full of rejection. A customer's initial reaction is almost always no. This builds insecurity, and many salespeople compensate by adopting a cocky, know-it-all attitude—particularly toward those who are not customers!

If this is a problem in your company, do not give in to it. Find creative ways to break through their facades and involve your top salespeople in figuring out how to get more business. Because of their direct contact with customers, salespeople can make a unique contribution to your planning meetings, and they can learn a lot about the problems and opportunities of the company at the same time.

Involving salespeople leads to
multi-million-dollar breakthrough

Everybody was happy with the plan we wrote after a Clinic at a small paging company. But business didn't increase. Each month dips and increases in income resulted in just breaking even. Management felt they had good salespeople. I kept asking the salespeople questions about the way the four stores operated, and solicited their suggestions. It became apparent that 60 to 70% of the salespeople's tasks were related to paper work, not selling. (In a talk at Inc. Magazine's Growing the Company Conference, Arthur Martinez, Chairman of Sears, talked about a study that showed that Sears retail salespeople were performing over 300 tasks, of which only 100 were directly related to selling. Martinez said that eliminating non-selling tasks had been critical to Sears' turnaround.)

We revamped paperwork systems and ran a series of Saturday morning sales training sessions in which we scripted phone conversations and created new closing programs. The results—a 2000% (yes, that's three zeros) increase in net additional customers per month. The company is now on its way to going public or being acquired. The owners will end up with millions of dollars in their pockets as a result of diagnosing and solving this problem.

Earlier I talked about owners, presidents, or CEOs who are, "or should be," involved in marketing and sales. Sometimes in entrepreneurial companies, especially startups, the founder is a technical person who came up with the original idea and would enjoy continuing on the R&D side. But there is nothing more important than customers, and often customers value dealing with the boss. They feel that working with the top person is one trade-off for the risk (or perceived risk) of buying from a small company. The story goes that Mrs. Fields herself made her company's first major cookie sale—to Neiman Marcus.

Of course, an owner or CEO meeting with customers is in a position to learn the customer's needs directly and act on them in ways that a large company generally cannot. Participating in sales may, therefore, put the owner or CEO in the best position to develop new products and services.

Even if your owner, president, or CEO is not on the planning team, the team might want to evaluate what their role in marketing and sales should be, and might want to include them in some of the meetings (for example in the session on strategy). You may also want to include the CFO—or whomever functions as the CFO—in the meeting on budget.

Owner leads planning team
from train wrecks to dentists

ETS—Environmental Transloading Services—was a hazardous waste hauler that specialized in cleaning up train wrecks. The current owner's father had started the company as a railroad salvage outfit 15 years before. The company had made money, but the new owner saw a significant opportunity if he could move the company into hauling the five waste streams from dental offices. That business had a higher margin and did not depend on train wrecks or tankers jackknifing on the freeway. The focus of ETS's first Clinic was to develop a marketing and sales plan and a business plan to take the company off the railroad tracks and into the dental suites.

How many players on your team?

Your planning team should include as many members as it takes to get the job done. For efficiency, even if your company is large, you probably don't want more than ten. If the company is so large that even its divisions are large, each division should have its own planning team, with coordination among them for company-wide issues such as overall strategy, image, Web site, and cross marketing.

If your company is relatively small, a team of between two and five people might be just right. What if you are a one-person startup, a virtual firm, or a professional making plans to expand your business? You can do the plan yourself. (It will still take only four hours a week, among other reasons because the number of doable opportunities is more limited.) Better, you can have a volunteer planning team. Even one or two additional people will help keep you committed and will add input and objectivity. Figure out which business associates, friends, and family members are interested in your success and qualified to be helpful, and ask them to join your marketing and sales planning team. Be ready to adjust your meeting schedule to their needs, and be prepared to return the favor.

Before you make your final decision as to who should be on the team, consider the implications for your company after the eight weeks is over and the plan is completed. The way working on a marketing and sales plan changed the dynamics among GBH's executives is instructive.

GBH defends prices, cuts costs—and creates team

GBH Distributing's sales of telephone headsets were growing fast. But, without a plan, the company competed primarily on price. Profits grew more slowly than revenue, and the rate of profit declined.

At a Dr. Revenue Marketing & Sales Clinic, GBH developed "The GBH Difference," a matrix of customer benefits that supported GBH's prices. In addition to avoiding price competition, GBH lowered marketing costs. They had traditionally mailed their catalog to over 30,000 customers and prospects. The new catalog was designed for insertion in Telemarketing Magazine, the industry leader. GBH got the new catalog out to over 50,000 potential users for less than the postage alone on the old catalog. A real push produced the catalog by the magazine's deadline. The result: an immediate 25% jump in sales, with profits increasing faster than revenue.

At GBH, the owner-president had been frustrated because although he and his staff came up with good ideas, they were rarely implemented. At the Clinic, the company's controller resolved long-standing problems of communication between the credit department and sales; the head of customer service coordinated with marketing and sales to make promotions work; the #1 salesperson stepped in at a critical point with a vital element of selling to large companies that he alone had learned from experience, and a newly hired salesperson was enabled to get a fast start in a remote territory. GBH's planning team evolved into an effective, ongoing executive committee.

3. Decide who should lead the team and whether to have a project administrator

The person responsible for marketing or sales is probably the most logical person to lead your team. This could be the VP or director of marketing or sales, or the owner, CEO, or president of the company. If the owner, CEO, or president currently leads marketing or sales but is transferring that role to another individual as the company grows, the new head of marketing or sales may be the perfect person to lead the planning process, with active participation by the current head.

Another possibility is for the heads of marketing and sales to be co-leaders of the team, functioning as a kind of executive committee between the weekly meetings of the full team. This can be a powerful way to keep things on track.

The team leader (or co-leaders) has overall responsibility for making sure that the team functions properly, that the meetings happen, assignments are carried out, and a plan is written and implemented. The leader chairs the meetings, except when he or she assigns another team member to chair a particular meeting or section of a meeting.

The team leader may want the assistance of a team administrator (TA). The TA creates and distributes agendas, collates data, sends reminders of assignments and meeting schedules, and may also follow up on assignments. The TA can be a member of the team or a staff person who is added to perform these tasks.

4. Decide whether to have an outside facilitator

This book is written as a do-it-yourself guide to the process I use when I lead a Dr. Revenue Marketing & Sales Clinic. But I would be remiss if I did not at least raise the possibility of using an outside facilitator. A good, experienced, knowledgeable outside facilitator can add objectivity and focus to your planning efforts, allowing you to accomplish more in less time. If you consider hiring an outside facilitator, make a thorough investigation of possible candidates before settling on two or three to investigate further. It is important to put serious time and effort into choosing a facilitator. One of the most important questions to ask a facilitator is this: "Do you agree that the planning meetings must produce a written marketing and sales plan for the coming year, with goals, a budget, and a calendar?" If so, exactly what role, if any, will the facilitator play in writing the plan? When I conduct a Dr. Revenue Marketing & Sales Clinic, I write a draft plan and deliver it within five business days after the Clinic. I'm not saying your outside facilitator has to write a draft of your plan, but you and the facilitator must know who is responsible for writing the plan.

Because marketing consultants tend to specialize in marketing, and sales consultants specialize in sales, it may be hard to find an outside facilitator who grasps the relationship between marketing and sales and feels comfortable dealing with them together.

To investigate the candidates on your short list, after they pass your interview process, call three companies they've worked with in the past two years, but not last week or even last month. You want to talk to people who have had time to evaluate the results in real life. Ask them if they actually wrote a plan, and what specific results they've had from implementing their plans. I advocate caution because the wrong outside facilitator can destroy your planning process and sour team members on trying again. Some consultants will jump on ideas you suggest without first encouraging you to analyze all your opportunities to see which you should be working on now. Some consultants may not adequately consider strategic considerations.

Some of the worst results I've seen occurred when companies used their CPA or lawyer as the outside facilitator. It seemed logical: the company had a good relationship with an objective, smart professional who understood their business and even helped them grow. The problem arose when the CPA or lawyer turned out to have little experience in marketing and sales, but to be quite opinionated about these areas. I know CPAs and lawyers who are competent marketing and sales consultants, particularly in their fields, so this is not a blanket condemnation. It is simply a warning.

If you want an outside facilitator to follow the *Profit Rx* planning method, be sure that he or she has read this book and feels comfortable with this approach. If you are hiring a consultant who intends to use his or her own method, be sure you are comfortable with it, believe in its merits, and are confident it will lead to a practical plan that your company can implement.

When looking for an outside facilitator, ask other entrepreneurs whose business success has earned your respect about their experience. Ask leaders of your trade association, chamber of commerce, or networking group. You can also check with local and national marketing associations, most of which have Web sites. The business school at a local university may also be a good source.

There is a large variation in consultants, and a large range of prices. Some consultants are primarily university professors who consult on the side, others are fulltime consultants, or, as in my case, consultants, speakers, and writers. You cannot draw any conclusions about how good an outside facilitator will be based solely on how they allocate their professional time, nor is their fee necessarily a clue. Some relatively low-priced consultants may do an excellent job, while some relatively high-priced consultants may not. Probably the lowest you can expect to pay for a qualified person is $100 an hour plus expenses. At the other end of the scale there are "celebrity" marketing consultants who get $25,000 for a day of their time. My fee structure is available on www.ProfitRx.com.

5. Decide who will actually write the plan

You can have eight great meetings, but to end up with a written plan, someone has to put their fingers to the keyboard. Here's our suggestion as to the least painful and most helpful way to handle the writing process:

Writing should take place after each meeting. It's more important to get it done quickly—say within 48 hours—than to make it polished. You are going to end up making changes in the light of subsequent meetings, and there is no point in polishing text that may end up greatly altered or not there at all. A rough draft is fine until all the meetings have been completed. Get it done and circulated to all team members so they have a chance to think about it before the next meeting.

The team leader can do this writing, or assign different team members to write up the results of different meetings. You may be fortunate enough to have a team member who likes to write and is good at it. Anoint that team member as the official scribe. The team leader may want to review the scribe's work and make any necessary changes or additions before copying and distributing.

Whoever acts as the scribe should take thorough notes. Take the notes on your laptop and you are halfway through your writing assignment before the meeting is over. You are faced with a reorganizing and condensing job rather than a writing job. It's much more fun to cut and paste than to build from scratch.

Once the eight meetings are over, the scribe puts all sections of the plan together, changing the earlier parts to reflect decisions made later if necessary. Now is also the time to edit for clarity, readability, and if possible to make sure that the passion and commitment come across. Once your plan is completed, it's not just for the team members. It's a tool that can guide and motivate your sales people and many others within your company. It can have a positive effect on suppliers, customers, investors, and strategic allies as well.

6. Explain the project to the team members

There is a saying that the most important ingredient of a good speech is a good introduction. A strong, favorable introduction motivates the audience to like the speaker and the speech, and to understand that their investment of time and concentration will help them in the future.

The same logic applies to recruiting the members of your planning team. Few business people jump at the chance to attend another meeting, let alone a series of meetings. Review the Introduction to this book, which describes the competitive advantage of having a written marketing and sales plan. Apply that material to the challenges facing your company, and use it to motivate team members to see that this series of meetings is like no other. It will enable your company—and your team members—to make great strides forward. As sales, market shares, and profits increase, team members will earn financial rewards as well as professional growth. Help people understand that it is an honor and an opportunity to be selected for the planning team, and not "just another meeting."

These points will be an important part of the Launch Meeting, but you may also want to have an individual discussion about them with each person you've selected. It may be too soon to go into detail, but you may want to get team members thinking about their particular assignments now. Make it clear to everyone selected that the importance of creating a marketing and sales plan requires mandatory on-time attendance at all meetings and assignments that must be completed on time. Remember those players you didn't necessarily want but were concerned about excluding? With a little bit of luck, they will excuse themselves when you make it clear that there is work involved and give them a gracious way out if their other responsibilities are too demanding.

You'll notice that we're including the information on team building in the book, which everyone who will actually be on the team can and should read, rather than putting it in a separate "leader's manual." That's because we believe that people who fully understand what's going on will produce the best results. Which sets us up for the following point:

7. Provide each team member with a copy of Profit Rx

You want each member to arrive at each meeting fully aware of the goal of that meeting, and prepared accordingly. The only way that can happen is for each member to have his or her own copy of this book, to read, mark up, and think about. The first benefit of selection for the planning team is being presented with a copy of *Profit Rx*. Urge everyone to read the Introduction that night, if not sooner. Create a buzz!

To get a book for each team member, visit www.ProfitRx.com or call 800-322-0258 to get the volume discount on orders of five or more. If this book helps you write and implement an effective marketing and sales plan, consider buying copies for your customers, distributors, suppliers…whomever could benefit. At Holiday time, they might appreciate a copy of *Profit Rx*, with an explanatory note from you about how it can add to their bottom line for the coming year, more than another gift basket or bottle of booze.

8. Assign responsibilities for the first meeting, and alert team members about upcoming assignments that require lead time

Everyone should read the Introduction and Chapter 1 before the first meeting. If they can read the whole book by then, they will be even more prepared to contribute to the creation of a valuable marketing and sales plan. They will understand the serious nature of this project, the work that's involved, and the benefits that will result. The more team members who take an active role from day one, the better your plan will be. Everyone should also complete *Dr. Revenue's Marketing & Sales Check-Up*. Copy it from pages 295-301 or use the interactive version on www.ProfitRx.com.

Everyone should copy the final "Results" section of the *Marketing & Sales Check-Up* and get it to the team leader or team administrator (whomever is designated) no later than 48 hours before the first meeting. The team leader will average the scores and distribute the composite results at the Launch meeting, and will review the three ideas for immediate improvement to see if there is a convergence of opinion or some other remarkable finding.

Everyone should pay particular attention to the competitive matrix (pages 83-88), and come to the Launch meeting prepared to discuss two questions to prepare your company's competitive matrix:

1. Who are your company's chief competitors?

2. What are the most useful parameters for comparing you to them?

Those involved in sales forecasting should begin preparing for the third meeting, where sales forecasts will be required. Frontline salespeople must play the leading role in making meaningful forecasts. They should forecast sales for the next 12-18 months for every customer that accounts for 2% or more of their revenue. Those team members who will be involved in making the forecasts or seeing to it that they are completed should read the relevant parts of Chapter 3 now (pages 120-128) and take action to get the process started. They should also do the checkup required to make sure that the forecasts arrive on time to be copied, distributed, and reviewed before the third meeting.

The team administrator (TA), if there is to be one, should be briefed on his or her assignments, and on the priority nature of the project. If other urgent tasks are going to interfere with timely completion of assignments for the Marketing & Sales Planning Team, the TA should immediately report the problem to the team leader, who will do what is necessary to solve the problem. If the team leader is unavailable, the TA should go to another team member who has been designated in advance.

The initiator of this project has had a head start, and may have concluded that taking certain steps now will prove helpful at a later stage of the planning process. So he or she may assign particular team members to investigate new alliances, new markets, new methods of production, new advertising or promotional concepts—whatever appears relevant and potentially doable. These assignments may range from a few hours on the Internet or the phone to hiring a research firm or reviewing trade publications. As all team members will see once they get into the planning process, you never know where it will take you or what doors it will open.

9. Decide where to meet

It is a great help in the planning process to post materials on the walls, from blowups of competitive matrixes to flip chart pages with lists of opportunities or problems to advertising demos. Charts of sales and profits, calendars, timelines, organization charts can all stimulate thinking. Therefore, if possible you should have a room dedicated to the marketing and sales planning project, where you can leave materials on the walls and/or the whiteboard, or even on the

conference table. Team members can visit the room between meetings to do their assignments or just to think in an atmosphere, away
from day-to-day responsibilities. If others must use the room between
planning meetings, they should be instructed to leave the exhibits
alone. Post notices to that effect to avoid slipups.

Many companies refer to this dedicated room as the "war room," in
recognition of the competitive nature of business and the all-out team
effort that produces victories. Even the need to make creative, timely
plans based on incomplete information is similar to war. But at a Dr.
Revenue Marketing & Sales Clinic I conducted for an entrepreneurial
company in southern California, "war room" clashed with the company's culture. I suggested "growth room." They decided on "greenhouse." This is not a gibe at Southern California, where I have enjoyed
living for many years, and which is home to more than its share of successful entrepreneurial companies. Call it your war room, growth
room, greenhouse, or, if the spirit moves you, concept cafeteria. The
point is that if you can dedicate a space to the planning project, it
helps.

Do not allow lack space to keep you from moving forward; some
great plans have been written by companies that hardly had room to
conduct their day-to-day operations. One company turned that problem into an advantage by renting a meeting room in a nearby hotel for
each of its eight weekly meetings, thus getting away from interrup-
tions, and underlining the importance of the project.

10. Decide when to meet

When to meet is more important than where to meet, but it can
depend on the availability of your location, thus its position on our
list. As we described in the Introduction, the basic method laid out in
this book is to have eight 4-hour planning meetings, one meeting a
week for eight weeks. We have supplied an agenda for each meeting
that allocates time so that each meeting takes four hours or less. Get
everybody together, with their calendars, and set the schedule for all
eight meetings. (As long as you can reach agreement on when to have

the first meeting, this step can be put off until then.) If you're in an industry where it's impossible to make commitments eight weeks ahead, schedule the first three or four meetings. Make it clear to all that each team member must prepare for each meeting, arrive on time, and plan to stay until the end.

You may already have regular meetings to discuss marketing and sales. Those can go on forever without producing a marketing and sales plan, because they are not designed for that purpose. To end up with a good plan, insist that the meetings outlined in this book are kept separate from all other company functions.

By working through these details you've demonstrated your commitment to writing a marketing and sales plan. Now, on to some equally necessary but perhaps more exciting material.

Know your competition

I used to be astonished at the lack of knowledge companies have about their competitors. Now, after working with over 400 companies, I'm astonished only when I find one that is knowledgeable about its competitors. Here's what I find is the norm:

- Retail managers who rarely, if ever, visit competing stores

- Manufacturers who rarely, if ever, analyze competing products

- Executives who rarely, if ever, visit their competitors' Web sites

- Marketing and sales people who go to trade shows and don't systematically collect and review competitors' marketing materials

I could go on, but you get the point.

There are two typical exceptions:

- People who used to work for a competitor. Their picture of their former employer is often frozen in time, one-sidedly negative. It's as if they escaped from a bad marriage and don't want to hear anything more about their spouse, especially anything good.

- Salespeople. They hear about their competition every day from customers and potential customers. Problem: All they hear is how great the competition is, and how low their prices are (and how terrible their own products are, and how high their prices are). The best salespeople figure out that if all this were true, the customers would have no reason to even be talking to them.

Competitive intelligence pays off

I was helping a graphic arts firm recruit top salespeople from the competition after we had canned four of ours who were not doing the job. I interviewed a cocky guy who was with one of the competitors. He had one major flaw, a couple of subtle weaknesses, and he talked too much! We did not hire him, but based on what I learned at the interview, we were able to devise a way for our salesperson to compete with him more effectively. During the next 12 months we more than doubled our rate of proposals closed when he was our primary competitor.

One of the simplest and least expensive ways to get an edge on your competitors is to take a little time to learn about them. The best way to study your competition is in relation to yourself. This gives focus and purpose to your information gathering, and as you will see in the next chapter, leads directly to opportunities for your company.

Build your competitive matrix

A competitive matrix is a simple but powerful tool for systematically evaluating your company's strengths and weaknesses relative to your competitors.

How does it work? Let's use a relatively simple example. My wife, Liz Haskell, is the founder and CEO of Country Faire Bakery. Country Faire bakes and sells cookies in West Los Angeles. When she started,

I urged Liz to develop a competitive matrix to help identify opportunities. Liz did not like this idea (to say the least). She said, "I'm a baker, not a market researcher." Finally she agreed to do the matrix, but only if I would do the tasting. Liz did not want to eat inferior cookies.

Competitive Matrix

Bakeries	Taste	Price	Location	Customer	Packaging
Country Faire Bakery	9	7	8	10	10
Bakery 1	7	8	6	8	8
Bakery 2	6	7	9	7	7
Bakery 3	7	9	7	7	7
Bakery 4	5	7	10	4	4
Bakery 5	4	8	6	6	6

To create the competitive matrix, we identified Liz's five main competitors and listed them in the left-hand column, along with County Faire. Next, we decided on the key parameters of competition and wrote them across the top of the matrix. The parameters vary from industry to industry. In our case, we decided they were taste, price, location, packaging, and "customer," by which we meant the level of customer affluence.

Next, we filled in the boxes by evaluating County Faire and its competitors in each parameter on a scale of one through ten, with ten being the best, and one being terrible. The scale often has to be further refined for each parameter. For example, in our competitive matrix,

- taste: 10 = fabulous; 1 = wretched

- price: measures only price, not value; therefore the higher the number, the lower the price (because we felt that high price alone was a negative)

- location: 10 = perfect for customer base, traffic, parking; 1 = inaccessible

- packaging: 10 = terrific professional packaging, several unique features (such as in Liz's case, the name of each type of cookie on sealed bag); 1 = throw cookies into an open generic bag

- customer: 10 = upscale, price no object; 1 = can't afford product

When constructing your own competitive matrix, it's hard to be objective. You may unconsciously want to select only those parameters that slant things your way. Try to look at every competitor—and yourself—through the eyes of a potential customer who has no prior allegiance. When you are putting yourself in the head of potential customers, you should also take into account that few if any customers have your knowledge of the industry.

At the Launch meeting, you're going to decide who your main competitors are, so give it some thought. In many instances, that's not as simple as it sounds. In Liz's case, for example, we decided that her main competitors were other "boutique" cookie bakeries, not supermarkets, nor even bakeries that created other products as well as cookies.

You may decide you have two or more distinct sets of competitors. For example, you manufacture and sell high-tech ceramics for scientific applications. You have only two direct competitors, but another group of competitors manufacture and sell similar products made from metal. Or, you sell office supplies from a superstore, and your direct competition is massively visible four blocks down the street. But you also know that you are competing against less visible but equally present mail order office supply catalogs. Another example, relevant to many consultants is this: You have three significant direct competitors, but the indirect competition is that the potential client can, or believes he can, do the job internally. Even more insidious indirect competition is that the potential client may decide not to do the job at all.

You may feel it would be useful to have two competitive matrixes: one that compares you with your direct competitors, and one that compares you with your indirect competition. These competitive matrixes would probably require at least some different parameters of comparison.

At the Launch meeting you will decide what parameters to use in comparing yourself to your competition—the equivalents of Liz's taste, price, location, packaging, and customer. So give that some thought as well.

How to get information about your competitors

If you've done applicable market research, you can use the results to fill out the competitive matrix. In fact, working on the competitive matrix may suggest areas for market research, which doesn't have to be time consuming or expensive. For example, I decided to share the glory (and calories) of my cookie tasting assignment by inviting a group of friends over for coffee and a blind cookie tasting.

Of course, if you are a salesperson, you've heard a lot about your competition from your customers and potential customers. If you're not a salesperson, ask your salespeople to tell you about the competition. The ones who are always on your customers' lips are certainly your direct competitors. Just realize that many customers tell you one-sidedly positive stories about your competition as a bargaining tactic. Also realize that horror stories about a competitor may not be typical of its performance.

Here's an example of how you could get information on your competitors if you operate a retail store. With a little imagination, you can develop tactics to get similar information about the competition in your industry. Their Web sites can be a great place to start.

Informal competitive research for a retail store

Identify as many stores as possible devoted exclusively to your product. Visit each store and pace off its size. This horseback measurement will give you very approximate square footage for each competitor.

Estimate the square footage of your own store by using the same pacing method, in order to compare apples to apples. Then, use your own sales figures for the past few years to estimate your dollar sales per square foot.

Visit the stores at a variety of times to estimate how busy they are, by counting the number of customers entering the store, the number of cars in its parking lot—whatever works. Also collect information on lines carried, prices, service, layout, décor, location, and so on.

Construct a matrix that includes your store and each competitive store, and enter its square footage in the "size" column. Create another column headed "volume/sq. foot." Rate your store 1.0. If a competitor appears to be doing about the same volume per square foot, it gets a 1.0. If a competitor appears to doing 25% more business per square foot than you, enter 1.25. Twenty-five percent less, enter 0.75. And so on. Now multiply the square footage by the volume/sq. foot factor and enter in another column the estimated total volume of each competitor relative to yours. (If you wish, enter your actual dollar volume and use the resulting ratio to estimate their dollar volumes.)

Make columns for all the categories of information you collected, and see if a pattern emerges that reveals what factors lead to higher volume per square foot.

(For stores that sell a broad range of items, like a K-Mart, pace off only the section of the store devoted to the merchandise you sell.)

Now that you've spent some time thinking about who your competitors are, and what the best parameters of comparison are, you're prepared for the Launch meeting. Before going to the meeting, please study the assignments and agenda. They are on page 40-43, or your team leader or team administrator may have given you a customized version. Also, review Dr. Revenue's Rules of Order, on page 39, which will help you get the most out of every minute you spend at any business meeting.

On to opportunities

Congratulations. With the competitors and the parameters filled in on your competitive matrix, you are off to a jump start on identifying opportunities for your company. That's the subject of the next chapter. And that's what you'll be doing at the Opportunities meeting, which is one of the most free-wheeling, exciting, and enjoyable meetings of the series.

Search for all opportunities to find the most rewarding ones. Those who win in business not only know how to think, they know what to think about.

CHAPTER 2

DISCOVER OPPORTUNITIES

Opportunities are the seeds from which the rest of your marketing and sales plan will grow. Analyzing opportunities leads to reality-based goals as opposed to goals based on wish-fulfillment. What's the difference? Suppose stockholders want more return on investment, so management calls for a 20% increase in sales and profits. Well, what is there about the company, the industry, and the period that make 20% growth possible? Or for that matter, why is the goal 20% and not 30%? Is the 20% increase expected to take place across the board (highly unlikely given the unevenness of change)? If not, what products, services, or areas will account for the major gains, and how much will they have to increase to pull the entire company up 20%? Finally, will your company's people buy into goals that appear to be plucked out of the air? Or are they more likely to be excited and motivated to work for goals that are based on analyzing real opportunities?

Now let's look at how an opportunity might lead to a reality-based goal. Say your present customers realize that one of your products is superior to those of your competitors. That's the opportunity. The problem is that your customers are clustered in your area of the country, a market you have almost saturated. You need to expand nationally. Potential customers outside your area are unfamiliar with your advantages and see only that your prices are higher than what they have been paying. You decide to seek endorsements from your present customers and use them as the basis of a marketing and advertising campaign that will get out the story of how you add value. Based on previous experience, you estimate that this campaign will produce 100 qualified responses, and that you will close one out of three. On the average, each sale will produce $50,000 during the first year, so the 33 deals will yield $1.65 million. Production people say they can turn out this much new product, but some overtime will be required. Present sales of this product are $3.3 million, so a reasonable goal from this campaign is a 50% increase in sales of this product. Production costs will be higher as a result of overtime, and your sales expenses will be higher because these will all be new customers and most will be out of your local area. You make estimates that result in a goal of increasing profit on this product through new customer sales by 30%, not 50%. Marketing, sales, and production people buy into these goals, beccause they participated in developing them and understand why and how they can be fulfilled.

By considering problems and goals, we have gotten ahead of ourselves with this example. Every opportunity comes with problems attached. If it didn't, it wouldn't be an opportunity anymore, but an accomplishment. And every opportunity logically leads to a goal.

Before thinking about problems and goals, though, we want to step back and investigate all our opportunities. The example we just looked at sounds like it's exactly the right thing to do. But what if the company has another product that brings in an average of $500,000 per sale, with higher margins and lucrative service contracts? And what if a similar campaign around that product could yield a $16.5 million increase in sales, instead of a $1.65 million increase? And what if the company doesn't have the resources to pursue both opportunities?

By searching for all opportunities, you find the most rewarding ones and avoid squandering time, energy, and money chasing opportunities with lower potential. Those who win in business not only know how to think, they know what to think about.

Opportunities galore

Unless you build stagecoaches (and possibly even then), you will probably find yourself awash with opportunities. When you completed the *Marketing & Sales Check-Up,* it probably did not take you long to think of three ideas for improving your marketing and sales programs immediately. Once you start brainstorming, it's relatively easy to come up with 10 or 20. But it's impossible to act on more than three or four at once. You don't have the budget, the people, or the time to focus on all your opportunities. That's why it's important to select the best opportunities, and save the others for possible action later.

If you are a 1-person operation, or a startup with a limited budget, you may be able to exploit only one opportunity in your first marketing and sales plan. That's fine. It's better to build success based on doing a great job with one opportunity than to chase five opportunities and get meager results because you have spread yourself too thin. Success in one opportunity yields the resources to capitalize on other opportunities.

Step one is to list your opportunities. That way, when you start the selection process, the best ones—or at least the best ones you discover—are on the list. Even a startup should come up with 5 or 10 opportunities; an established company might find 20 or more. (If you are working on a marketing and sales plan for a division, a product line, or a product, the same logic applies.)

At this stage, it's counterproductive to think about the problems attached to the opportunities, or even to try to quantify their outcomes. Instead, let your creativity and imagination run wild. Brainstorm. The team should take a non-judgmental approach. No one should find it necessary to introduce an opportunity by saying, "I know this is a crazy idea, and we'd never have the budget for it, and our distributors would never buy into it, but…." Defensiveness and inhibitions can leave the best opportunities as mere wisps of thought inside your head. Say the words aloud and they may click with something a colleague has been holding in that could lead to a quick small gain...or the biggest breakthrough in company history. Spit out the opportunities; save the critiques and comparisons for the selection process.

Use Section III of *Dr. Revenue's Marketing & Sales Check-Up* and your Competitive Matrix to help you envision your opportunities.

When should you stop looking for opportunities?

Levi Strauss & Co., founded in 1850, is the world's largest brand-name apparel maker, with 1996 sales of $7.1 billion. Yet, in October, 1997, the company announced that it was laying off 6,400 workers, or one third of its work force. Its market share in men's jeans had declined from 31% in 1990 to 19% in 1996. Lower-priced store brands had cut away part of their market, higher-priced designer labels another part.

Levi Strauss is a great company and may well, like Chrysler, make a great comeback. But the lesson is clear: No matter how successful you are, never stop looking for opportunities. The external environment in which you function changes constantly, so unless you continuously search for opportunities, you operate in the past. That's a sure formula for failure. Especially when smaller competitors, with less inertia to overcome, can change faster.

Finding opportunities

The opportunity that God sends
does not wake up him who is asleep
—Senegalese proverb

An opportunity is an advantage that allows you to make your sales and profits grow. By working on an opportunity, you control your destiny. You drive the situation, making things happen rather than waiting for the phone to ring.

Even after you analyze your Competitive Matrix, it is not always apparent how the information you've assembled translates into opportunities for your company. The following questions and examples, which correspond to Section III of *Dr. Revenue's Marketing & Sales Check-Up*, may stimulate your thinking.

1. Do you have products or services with demonstrably superior quality?

Price is of course important in today's competitive environment. Sometimes sales people, under constant pressure, conclude that lowering their prices is the only way to make the sale. But it's not. If it were, nobody but the lowest priced provider would be in business. In real life, the lowest priced provider is at least as likely to go out of business. "Remember People's Express" would be a good slogan to use when surrounded by associates who advocate lowering your price as the only way to compete. (For those under 30, People's Express was a no-frills airline with rock-bottom fares. They had a huge terminal at Newark Airport, and were fantastically successful at filling their cramped seats. Their only problem: they lost money on every ticket they sold. Sales grew and grew until their bank account hit empty. Then People's Express flew right off the airline industry's Competitive Matrix.)

Why do people pay a premium for a superior product? Suppose you install local area networks. You demonstrate that your LAN is far less likely to fail than your competitors' installations. Your prospect, a community bank, is involved in the fierce competition of the banking industry. Which do you think the bank is more concerned about: shaving 10% off the price of the network, or having to tell customers, "Our system is down"?

On the consumer front, you may own a Sub Zero brand refrigerator. Sub Zeros have features that are supposed to keep food fresher, such as constant air circulation and doors that automatically lock until a safe temperature is re-established. Some models allow you to slide in panels to match your kitchen decor. Sub Zero buyers pay a hefty premium for these features—and for the status of ownership.

Customers who buy high-end products and services want the best, or the fastest, or the latest. They value their time, convenience, and peace of mind, and are willing to pay a premium. An edge in this direction opens many opportunities. Looking ahead to tactics, you could, for example,

- increase prices

- attract high-end distribution channels

- attract quality strategic partners

- win awards from industry publications and associations

All of the above, even a relatively high price, can further enhance your reputation for quality and keep customers happy to pay a premium. Higher margins can also provide more revenue for R&D, which can help maintain and expand your lead in quality.

You might even be able to use your reputation for quality to penetrate beyond the high end of your market, by making serviceable, lower-cost products. A number of California wine makers became known for their high quality Napa Valley varietals, then used the prestige of their labels to sell lower-priced wines to the mass market. Clothing and shoe companies open factory outlets that sell seconds or discontinued items. The trick is to increase your market share without undermining the appeal of the high-end products that are basic to your success.

2. Do you provide unique services which differentiate your company from your competitors?

If you are you a Hertz Number One Gold member, you find your name up in lights, go directly to your rental car and drive away—no stopping at a counter, no waiting in line. To consistently receive this special treatment you have to pass up shopping for the lowest price and you may have to pay a $49 annual fee (often waived for frequent renters). Is it worth it? Thousands of business travelers think so, and therefore, don't shop around. Imagine the value of this repeat business to Hertz, which has based an advertising campaign around its Number One Gold program.

Another travel example: When you leave your own car at the airport, the parking service may offer to wash and wax it while you are away. They get double or triple what you would pay at a regular car wash. But isn't it convenient to come home to a sparkling clean car— and to avoid a separate trip to a car wash?

A business writing firm, in addition to its normal services, offers overnight editing of documents sent to them on-line.

A distributor of industrial chemicals developed a customer base among small manufacturers by accepting orders for smaller quantities than their competitors, and delivering within 24 hours, at an additional charge.

These additional services develop customer loyalty and therefore permit increased margins on the basic product or service. In our examples they create an additional profit center as well. In the case of the chemical distributor, the extra services turned a commodity product into a unique product.

If you provide a unique service along with your basic product, you have the opportunity to stand out from your competitors and attract and retain more customers without competing primarily on price.

3. Does your company have a different/better reputation, history, or market position?

Suppose you are the first to enter the market with a new product or service that fills a previously unsatisfied need? Until your competitors catch up, you have a window of opportunity. If you take advantage of it, you can expand rapidly based on your monopoly position.

AVT charges ahead

AVT, a small manufacturer of battery assemblies and battery chargers based in the Denver area, developed "smart integrated battery chargers." Smart chargers bring a rechargeable battery to its optimum charge much more reliably than typical "dumb chargers," in a fraction of the time. Products run longer between charges, and batteries last longer because they are not overcharged or overheated. AVT offers customized smart chargers and battery assemblies to OEMs (Original Equipment Manufacturers). They are using their technological lead to break out of their Rocky Mountain States market and become a national and international force in their industry.

Being first creates an opportunity, but not a slam dunk. Business history is replete with companies that were first to market, then lost out to a company that could supply the need better, cheaper, or with more marketing muscle. SyQuest and others produced portable hard drives for personal computers for years before Iomega entered the market with its ZIP drive. Yet, through a combination of features, price, and marketing ability, Iomega's ZIP appears (at least for the moment) to have become the standard. Iomega drives are now included as original equipment by most manufacturers of PCs. This, of course, gives Iomega a literally built-in market for its ZIP disks.

Sometimes a long history of reliability and of standing behind your products can be decisive. A buyer may be tempted by the features and prices offered by a relatively new player in the PC market, but wonder if the company will be in business in two years. Buyers want security, and "Nobody ever got fired for buying IBM."

Mail order firms such as L.L. Bean and Lands End unconditionally guarantee to repair or replace their products for as long as you own them.

What about offering the lowest price? Staples and Office Depot are known for providing the same goods as your local office supply store, but at far lower prices. In addition, they have a wider variety and are open longer hours.

Whether you are first, big, established, low priced, offer a superior warranty, or are small and quick to react, there is something about your company's position which leads to opportunity.

4. Do you have competencies which differ from competitive firms?

Century City in Los Angeles is full of law firms. At first glance, they appear more the same than different. Closer analysis reveals that some are full-service firms that can handle all your legal needs; others specialize in one area, such as real estate, intellectual property, or estate planning; some emphasize the relatively low cost of their services; and others tout their deep knowledge and experience.

A firm that emphasizes cost effectiveness may see an opportunity to grow among startups and small and mid-size clients with limited budgets. A "superstar" firm may see its growth opportunities among big, cash-rich companies with high value at stake.

Suppose you are considering hiring a PR firm. One large firm tells you they can represent you globally and have an international database of reporters, including when they want to be called, their deadlines, and whether they prefer to receive phone calls, faxes, or email. A local boutique firm tells you they have lower overhead, and therefore lower prices, and they specialize in your industry, and therefore have greater insight and more relevant contacts. What would you do? Probably, get more information. But you can see that each firm has a selling position that creates opportunities for itself.

5. Are you in a rapidly growing market?

Seattle has a local TV show similar to "Saturday Night Live." In its spoof news segment, it did a feature on "the last street corner in Seattle without a latté cart." If demand in your industry is growing rapidly, as it is for gourmet coffee throughout the United States, that can be a great opportunity for you. As with all of these categories, it's not a sure thing. You may be unable to increase production quickly enough to take advantage of the demand, or strong new competitors may flock into your market. Those are the problems to consider later. For now, the question is what kinds of opportunities does the growth present? For example, could you focus on higher margin products and services? On bigger customers? On developing a new territory?

Manufacturing a window of opportunity

A Minneapolis window treatment dealer was growing fast through good marketing into increased demand. In addition to its retail business, the company also manufactures window treatments, such as wood blinds. The manufactured products were sold primarily through the company's own retail operation, and the manufacturing side of the business was looked on as less exciting and important than the retail side. As a result, manufacturing had received little marketing attention, even though it produced quality products that were potentially highly competitive and profitable.

Opportunities arise in strange ways. Once management paid attention, the neglect of the manufacturing operation became an opportunity. Why not make manufacturing a separate division? With its own marketing and sales organization, manufacturing could focus on selling its products through new outlets, far enough from the company's retail center so as not to cannibalize sales. The plant already had the capacity to produce more product than the retail operation could handle, and the products were already proven, so this was a relatively low risk/high potential opportunity. Note also that it could be tested, by present personnel or by hiring one sales person part-time or on a temporary basis, before being fully implemented.

6. Are there products/services you do not presently provide that you could provide to the customers you now serve?

First of all, how do you know? Even if you come up with what seems to be a great idea, will it really work? The best way to find out if you can supply an additional product or service is to ask your customers. It has to be something they want, and something that they want to get from you. If you have developed close relationships with your customers, and they see you as a partner and problem solver, they are likely to tell you even without your asking them. The trick is for those in contact with customers to be listening so carefully that they hear what they are being told, and for your organization as a whole to be responsive to that input. We've mentioned AVT before. Their development of the smart integrated battery charger was very much a function of listening to the wants and needs of customers who were already buying battery assemblies from AVT. Similarly, customers of a gardening and landscaping service frequently asked for referrals to an exterminator when ants invaded their homes. After years of making referrals, the landscaping added pest extermination to its range of services.

7. Is your sales force uniquely qualified or well positioned to sell more?

There are many ways to sell: a field sales force, a store or showroom, an 800-number with "operators standing by," a Web site, direct mail, reps, and more.

They are all expensive. More so every year.

If you can get more sales out of your sales force for every dollar you put in, it's like getting more miles per gallon from your car. Other things being equal, it shows up on your bottom line.

We see an example of this every time we buy a major appliance for our homes. The sales person offers us a service contract. He or she is uniquely positioned to do so.

For every desk there is a...

Our family office furniture business, Haskell of Pittsburgh, Inc., was a well established source for desks, tables, and files, but we did not manufacture chairs. Nevertheless, every time someone bought one of our desks, they needed a chair—and of course they asked our reps to supply it. Our reps (Multiple-line Manufacturers Representatives) sold other manufacturers' chairs to go with our desks. We supported the concept of multiple-line selling through independent manufacturers' representatives, but we realized that we were giving these chair manufacturers a windfall. We bought a chair factory and learned the chair business. Within a few years we established our chairs as part of our package and we required every Haskell rep to drop his or her other chair lines and carry only Haskell chairs.

A Workers Comp insurance carrier or broker might decide its sales force was well qualified and well positioned to sell safety equipment or ergonomic solutions. A driver education service might sell car insurance. A ski resort might transform itself into a year-round resort without adding a sales person. Once you see the opportunity presented by having a sales force in place, there are many ways to take advantage of it. You might, for example, put your brand name on related products and services supplied by others. Or you might form a partnership with a complementary company in a different region that needs representation where you are, and vice versa. Or sell another company's software along with your hardware. Anything that meets your customers' needs and increases the efficiency of your sales force is an opportunity.

8. Is your company particularly well financed?

You don't want to waste money just because you have it, but money can open many doors. If there is a race to be first to market with a new product, you can afford the overtime, the additional staff, the consultants, the new equipment. And once the product is out, you can market it heavily. You can even build market share by selling it at a price that won't be profitable until large scale and/or offshore production kicks in. You may even scare less wealthy competitors from entering the market.

Cash reserves cut time to market
I was working on the marketing and sales program for Anderson Desk. Darryl Anderson, the president and

one of the owners of the company, asked me to take a look at a new, walnut-finish version of a desk that we had been making in oak for about a year. Sales of the oak model, called Encina, were high and growing each month. Darryl and I looked at the walnut-finish prototype. We thought it would sell.

Normally, the next steps would have been market research and test marketing. We decided that because sales had been strong and cash reserves were high, we could avoid these delays. "Let's get it in stock, do the literature, and see what happens. Probably the worst case is that we close out the initial run at cost." We had a winning basic desk design, and we had the financial structure to support the gamble. We won big-time. Soon the new Windsor model was selling just as well as the Encina, and we had not cannibalized our own product. We had carved out a larger share of market for Anderson Desk. An interesting feature of this example is that because Anderson Desk could afford the risk, it ended up saving the money it would have spent on market research and test marketing.

9. Do your vendor/customer relationships provide unique/special opportunities for current or new products?

You may be able to do cooperative marketing with your vendors or distribution channels, where you assist each other with advertising costs. A supplier may be in a position to give you good terms, such as net 90 or net 180, so that you can leverage up-front dollars to get new products and services going. Or, you may be able to give those terms to a distributor or end-user to make your products or services more attractive.

When you work with another company to offer a total solution, such as a hardware and software package, you may be able to market and sell as a partnership. This can involve joint sales calls, marketing literature that augments yours, and use of the partner's logo for added credibility. Microsoft, IBM, and Lotus, among others, have formal partnership programs.

Your staff may be eligible for sales and marketing training from suppliers. Or suppliers may be willing to contribute to the cost of a direct-mail piece, or contribute a mailing list they already have. You may never know until you ask. Some of your suppliers may have programs that publicize the success of selected customers (UPS, for example). Who gets selected? Call your story to their attention and you increase the odds in your favor.

Your outside professionals—bankers, accountants, lawyers, insurance brokers, marketing people, and other consultants—can introduce you to potential customers. This will happen only if you take the time to sell them—and resell them—on your company and your products and services. If, after doing that, you are still not receiving marketing and sales help from your outside professionals, look for replacements. These people have a vested interest in your success; if they don't get it, find professionals that do.

Suppliers sell you the products and services you need. Distributors sell your products and services to end users. But if that's the limit of your relationships, you—and they—lose out on opportunities. Develop the habit of thinking creatively about vendors and distributors as sources of opportunities, and you open up endless veins of gold for your business to mine. And think about bringing opportunities to your suppliers and distributors. The more you help them, the more they should be inclined to help you.

Carpet manufacturer agrees to cover retailer's warranty

In 1995 I was working with Carpeteria, a 77-store chain of carpet retail stores. The dominant player in carpet manufacturing is Shaw Mills. Shaw had already developed its Trustmark® system of selling and was aggressively pushing it into retail outlets with substantial marketing, advertising, and sales budgets.

The owners of Carpeteria did not want Shaw to dominate their sales floors and drive their marketing and sales efforts. We developed a Carpeteria warranty system that started from the Trustmark® concept, but which we felt was simpler and more user friendly. Shaw's support for the program was fundamental. By showing Shaw that Carpeteria was important to them as a customer, and that Carpeteria's program would move a lot of their carpet, Shaw was won to support the Carpeteria program.

10. Do you have new product research and development capabilities that are superior to other firms in your industry?

When potential customers know you are ahead in R&D, it gives them a reason to team up with you over the long term, removing you from a commodity position in which you compete only on price. You can and should tell customers about your superior R&D, but showing them is even better. Take them on a tour of your research facility and let them see the engineers, designers, chemists...whomever...at work. (Be careful not to leak sensitive information.) Talk about how you could develop a new...whatever...for them. If you are a small operation, the equivalent might be introducing a customer's engineer to your engineer, and letting them develop a personal relationship over lunch.

To take full advantage of your superior R&D capability, establish strong communication between your sales and marketing people and your technical people. That way you become a market-driven company that can jump on a customer need when your sales people discover it.

Non-nerd techie creates opportunities

Star Graphic Arts, a mid-size prepress (film) house in San Francisco, was fortunate enough to have a director of R&D who lived on the cutting edge of Silicon Valley technology—and was easy and enjoyable to work with. Customers loved to explain their needs to Peter. Peter and his team would develop solutions that lowered the customer's costs or response time, while increasing Star's margin and the quality of its relationship with the customer.

11. Do you have market superiority over your competition in the minds of your customers? Their customers?

Would you rather have a prospect who is thinking about buying, or one who has definitely decided to buy, and the only remaining question is to buy from you or from your competition?

If prospects believe you are the best in the field, always frame the question as though the only decision is to buy from you or a competitor. When you put the question that way, it helps a prospect see it that way. It's like the old, "Do you want it in red or blue?" rather than "Do you want it at all?" Of course, you would not want to do this if your product or service is not right for the prospect. If you do make the sale, you also make an enemy that could cost you lots of sales down the line.

Auto advertising is almost entirely along the lines of "Which?" rather than "Why?" Each manufacturer focuses on an area of actual or perceived superiority. Nobody pushes the general idea that cars are a really great way to get to work and visit friends and family. But if you are marketing a new product or service, you will probably have to sell people primarily on the general story. Ideally, once they understand why they will benefit from what you're offering, they'll buy it from you because you are the story teller who has enlightened them.

Returning to auto ads as an example, there are two ways to go in claiming superiority. You can just talk about how good you are, or you can make comparisons with your primary competitors.

If you are clearly perceived by most people as the market leader, you may be better off not publicizing the competition. If you have an edge, but many people don't know it, you may want to use direct comparisons to create market superiority in the minds of your customers.

12. Do you have a superior management team?

A CEO leaves a publicly traded company, or a new CEO is hired. The stock dips or jumps, although nothing else has changed. Why? Because investors recognize that over a period of time, leadership is everything. They've seen countless examples of great companies dragged down by poor leadership and companies near death turned around by great leadership. Chrysler in the 1980s is a good example of the latter; Apple Computer in the 1990s may be an example of both.

Your company's superior leadership is a marketing and sales advantage—if your potential customers know it, and understand how it helps them.

How can you let your customers know?

- Broadcast the reputation and resumes of your managers.

- Establish their expertise by placing articles by or about them in appropriate business and trade journals.

- Bring your CEO, president, CFO, VP of engineering—whatever works—into the sales process.

How will your customers understand that they will benefit?

- Managers can brief them on industry trends, one-on-one, in seminars, or in writing. (Potential danger: wrong predictions.)

- Managers in the sales process can apply their expertise to solve problems for the customer, so that they understand the value you add and why your product or service is the most cost effective. (Potential danger: undermining frontline troops.)

- Customers see that your managers have a long history of superior service and integrity. This is especially critical where trust is a big issue, as for example in banking, investment management, product safety, and health care.

Management pros seize new bit

In the mid-80s Zephyr Manufacturing, a manufacturer of aerospace tools, was owned by a holding company, Standun Corporation. Standun's president, Hal Rice, was the former managing partner of Arthur Anderson in Los Angeles. The President of Zephyr was Frank Sax, the former president of Abbey Rents and a true operations and research genius. Bernie Kersulis, Zephyr's Vice President for Finance and Administration, was a former Arthur Anderson manager and a financial wizard.

Such a high powered management team gave Zephyr a significant edge over the other small companies who were its competitors. Zephyr's hard-nosed managers were used to dealing with planning and numbers, and could separate wishes from reality. They were also good at listening to customers and suppliers, then analyzing how to take advantage of what they heard. One of many examples: Phillips (of Phillips screws) developed a new screwdriver bit which had special slotting to make it more resistant to torquing out. Zephyr management saw an opportunity to broaden their market by becoming a licensee for this product. They knew they had to support their new bits with aggressive advertising and promotion. They ran the numbers and saw a good chance for a high profit opportunity to sell the new bits and to attract customers to their whole line. They developed a successful marketing campaign for the new bits, around the slogan "Test drive a Z" (for Zephyr). Getting samples of the new high torque bits into users hands drove "Z" to high volume, fast!

From many opportunities to the best opportunities

Sometimes an entrepreneur will try to attract venture capital by demonstrating how many applications there are for a new product or service. It rarely works. Most VCs know that tight focus is an ingredient of success, and that spreading yourself too thin is a formula for failure.

You've come up with at least five opportunities, and more likely 20 or more. It takes attention, energy, time, and often money to pursue each opportunity. Human resources and budget are limited, so you cannot take advantage of all your opportunities at once. If you are a startup or a 1-person operation, you may be able to go after one or two. If you are a more established, larger organization, perhaps three or four.

How do you decide which opportunities to pursue now?

First, you've got to shift gears.

Until now, you were brainstorming, uncritically trying to come up with as many opportunities as you could.

Now is the time to get hard nosed and analytical.

Opportunities: Best, Worst, and Other

Best Low Risk High Potential	***OK but why bother?*** Low Risk Low Potential
Acceptable if you can afford it High Risk High Potential	***Worst*** High Risk Low Potential

The best opportunities: low risk with high potential

The best opportunities are those with low risk and high potential. Look for small changes that, with little or no investment, can yield big returns. If a small test can give a quick indication of whether the effort will succeed, better yet.

Test telephone marketing: no cost, big payoff

Little Earth makes fashion accessories from recycled materials. In creating their marketing and sales plan, we decided on a small change: take telephone marketing out of the company and contract with an outside, professional telemarketer to sell the displays to stores. The risk was small: internal telephone marketing had not proven viable. Little Earth was too small to give it a meaningful test without committing too much money. The telemarketer used high level people who would not alienate potential customers and was paid only from revenue they produced. The potential payoff was large: if telephone marketing worked, the outside contractor could quickly put a lot of experienced people on the phones and develop huge incremental volume.

The worst opportunities: high risk with low potential

The worst opportunities are those with high risk and low potential. Say, for example, you have the opportunity to increase sales by making more sales calls that require flying to other cities, renting cars, hotel accommodations, and so on. The sales cycle for this product typically requires two visits over a period of six months. When you do finally make a sale, the operating margin is $2000. Even if the plan works, it yields little or no profit after sales expenses.

Rule out high risk, low potential opportunities. They are opportunities for loss. This point seems so obvious as to be hardly worth stating. Yet, many companies have wasted many millions of dollars on this kind of marshmallow marketing.

The other opportunities

What kinds of opportunities are left? High risk, high potential and low risk, low potential.

A high risk, high potential opportunity is acceptable if

• you can afford to take the risk

• and/or you cannot afford not to take the risk

• it doesn't preclude your best low risk, high potential opportunity

For example, you are an up-and-coming player in your niche and you recently picked up some major orders at the annual trade show. You were overshadowed there, though, by the large, well-staffed exhibit of your biggest, best known competitor. You've got a few million dollars in the bank. You decide to spend $150,000 on a new exhibit for next year's show, and another $150,000 on more space at the show and bringing more staff. Your analysis is that a larger more sophisticated presence will help establish you as a top-level competitor, opening the way for the biggest orders. And that if you continue your lower-level presence, you won't be able to advance. The trade show display does not have to be a one shot event. It can be the keystone of your new, more aggressive approach to high-end marketing and selling. If the tactic fails, you're out 300K, but if it succeeds, you're up $millions and playing in a new league.

What about low risk, low potential opportunities? In theory, they are acceptable if they don't preclude high potential opportunities, but in real life, why bother planning for such low payoffs? If you've done a good job of coming up with opportunities, there should be at least three or four with high potential. Concentrate on them.

Daddy, what do you do?

Do you provide a service? Is it as hard for potential clients to grasp the benefits as it is for your kids? A small (low cost, low risk) change that can yield big results is to "productize" your deliverable. For example, I am a marketing and sales consultant. "So what do you do?" was often the question, meaning, "How can you help me?" I came up with "Dr. Revenue's Marketing and Sales Clinic," a 1-day program that leads to a draft marketing and sales plan delivered within five working days. Now the reaction from a potential client is more often, "Oh, I see." Look at the Clinic 1-sheet on pages 114 and 115. The product is quickly defined and described on the front. The back provides the details, so the prospective client has a chance to "kick the tires." Everything is spelled out: what you will get, why you will benefit, who's giving it, the cost, the guarantee.

Select at least one low-risk, high-potential opportunity that is likely to yield results relatively quickly, to generate revenue for other activities and to validate your planning process. If you have the forces to pursue them simultaneously, select two.

Hold the problems

In selecting opportunities to pursue now, try not to worry about the problems involved in achieving them. Assume that all opportunities can be taken advantage of, and select those that seem to have the greatest return on investment and fastest market impact. You'll be discussing problems and how to overcome them once you have decided on which opportunities to pursue. There is a feedback loop. If it turns out that a problem appears insurmountable or too costly to correct, you will scrap that opportunity and select another one. Therefore be sure to keep a record of all the opportunities, even those you don't select as the best.

The role of consensus in selecting opportunities

The owner or head of the division is ultimately responsible for performance. So after the potential and the risks of each opportunity are evaluated, shouldn't he or she select the ones to pursue?

Probably not. It's much better if it can be done by consensus, for two reasons. First, if the key people don't agree with the person in charge, there's a good possibility the decision is wrong. Second, even if it's correct in the abstract, if the people who have to implement it don't agree, there is almost no chance the decision will be carried out well. Most people can be enthusiastic, creative, and dedicated only when they agree with a course of action, or at least don't strongly disagree with it.

Consensus works only if each team member expresses his or her true thoughts, questions, anxieties, and doubts. Good managers are aggravated when people who could have helped make a better decision don't come forward at the critical moment. Yes-men/women subvert the opportunity-selection process. If you are in charge, do

Sales sluggish?
Marketing out of focus?

Call Dr. Revenue for a Guaranteed* Cure!

JOHN HASKELL
Dr. Revenue
Rx for a Healthy Business

- WRITTEN SALES & MARKETING PLAN 5 DAYS POST CLINIC
- DR. REVENUE BECOMES YOUR SHORT-TERM CMO (CHIEF MARGIN OFFICER)
- INSTALL HIGH-IMPACT SALES SYSTEMS — SALES ↑
- PROFITS ↑

Next Appointment
DO NOT SUBSTITUTE

Call Dr. Revenue for an on-site clinic and watch your marketing and sales strategy snap into focus. Dr. Revenue (aka John Haskell) has 25 years experience helping management of entrepreneurial companies create sustained profitable growth. He's written over 300 marketing plans and is a frequent speaker for Inc. Business Resources seminars.

Call 800-332-0258 today for detailed information about the **Marketing & Sales Clinic** (available in 1-1/2, 1 and 1/2 day formats). **Ask for your FREE audiotape,** *Building a Marketing Plan Step by Step*.

What do patients say about Dr. Revenue's clinics?

"The headline says it all — 'Aggressive Marketing Saves Company' (Los Angeles Daily News). For myself and my family, thank you."
Bruce A. Moss, President, **Artwood Desk Design**

"Your material continues to be the leading component of all our presentations. It's still making the dynamic impression it did five years ago."
Carey Brazell, President, **Myers Brazell & Associates**

"Our volumes are increasing steadily and our revenue per unit of sales is at levels not seen in years."
Todd Hoffman, Vice President Sales & Marketing, **Lykes Meat Group**

DR. REVENUE'S
Marketing & Sales Clinic

60 East Chestnut, Suite 253
Chicago, IL 60611
Phone: 800.332.0258
Fax: 219.923.3603
eMail: DrRevenue@DrRevenue.com

* Guarantee: Hold a Dr. Revenue *Marketing & Sales Clinic* and within six months you will get increased sales equal to at least five times your investment — or your money back.

The Six Step Process

1) Dr. Revenue reviews your information.

2) Key staff complete Dr. Revenue's pre-clinic questionnaire.

3) Dr. Revenue leads a 12-14 hour Marketing and Sales Clinic for your team.

4) Five days after the Clinic, Dr. Revenue delivers your draft Marketing Plan with clear written directions for completion in 60 days.

5) You receive a Dr. Revenue Sample Marketing Plan with guidelines for completion of your plan plus an audio tape - Building a Marketing Plan Step by Step.

6) Dr. Revenue meets with your team once a week for 6 weeks by phone to help complete the plan.

DR. REVENUE'S Marketing & Sales Clinic

- Fast cost-effective action
- Focused results
- Draft Marketing & Sales Plan in 5 days
- Complete Marketing & Sales Plan in 60 days
- On-site one or one and a half day intensive program

Dr. Revenue/John Haskell is a frequent speaker at events sponsored by INC. Magazine. He holds a bachelor degree from Brown University and an MBA in Marketing from Kellogg School/-Northwestern University. After a successful career at companies including Eastman Kodak and Sara Lee Corp, Haskell founded The Professional Marketing Group, which served the marketing needs of small and medium sized companies for eleven years.

Dr. Revenue's Clinic starts with a thorough analysis of your business, and results in a complete detailed written sales and marketing plan. The focus is how to increase your sales, market share, and profits. The Marketing & Sales Clinic is your opportunity to pull together your team with the assistance of an expert leader.

Dr. Revenue's Detailed Clinic Cures

See results in just two days. In 60 days your company will have a focused, effective plan to generate higher sales and increased profits.

CREATING AND IMPLEMENTING A REWARDING MARKETING PLAN
Analyze past and current written marketing plans • Avoid repetition of past mistakes • Create a plan with the right basis

DATA YOU NEED FOR YOUR BUSINESS TO SUCCEED
Gather statistical data on your market • Organize your sales figures according to market data • Analyze market share

IDENTIFY AND RESOLVE PROBLEMS
Product quality • Service • Specific customers or prospects • Pricing • Sales force • Sales methods • Range of offerings • Competition

IDENTIFY AND LEVERAGE OPPORTUNITIES
Product superiority • Unique services • Company reputation and history • Solid financing • R&D capabilities • Perceived market superiority

ESTABLISH SALES GOALS/FORECASTS
Set quantified sales and profit goals • Sales forecasts for customers • Forecasts for all sales personnel by territory

ADVERTISING
Create an advertising plan • Get value for your advertising dollar • Measure advertising effectiveness • Provide your sales force, re-sellers, and customers with complete, effective sales tools

MERCHANDISING
Merchandising assistance to help you sell your products • Promote your company's abilities to customers • Assemble a complete, written, merchandising program

PUBLIC RELATIONS/PROMOTION
Assess PR's importance to your business • Use PR to increase profit • Set PR calendar • Notify sales people and customers in advance • Use promotions to create competitive advantage

MANAGING THE PLAN
Implementation program • Assign responsibility for each phase • Establish budget/control system • Milestone chart • Employee buy-in

REVIEW SYSTEM
Monitor specifics at all times • Reporting systems to assess impact • Actual vs sales vs forecasted sales analysis

Clinic Offerings

We charge our clients only once; clinic fees include all materials, travel and lodging, and 6 weeks of follow-up conference calls with your team.

One and 1/2 day clinic . . $15,000
One day clinic $10,000
1/2 day clinic $8,000

Satisfied clients include:

Asics Corp.	KPMG Peat
Carpeteria	Marwick
GBH Distributing	Marco Fireplaces
IBM	Price Waterhouse
Lykes Meats, Inc.	Toshiba

Call us for references, or to discuss Clinic Offerings and any special needs you might have.

John S. Haskell/Dr. Revenue
Professional Marketing Consultant
60 East Chestnut, Suite 253
Chicago, IL 60611
Phone: 800.332.0258
Fax: 219.923.3603
eMail: DrRevenue@DrRevenue.com
http://www.drrevenue.com

Guaranteed! *Hold a Dr. Revenue Marketing & Sales Clinic and within six months you will get increased sales equal to at least five times your investment — or your money back.*

everything in your power to discourage subservience and promote independent thinking. It's also important that each person keep an open mind and realize that reasonable people may have reasonable differences. Keep the dialogue issue-related rather than personal. Marketing is not an exact science. Your point of view and the opposite point of view may be equally logical. They may even be equally wrong. Some answers just cannot be known until they are tested.

Even if you are a 1-person show, you can get consensus. And it's important to do so. After selecting the opportunities to pursue, go over your reasoning with several business associates, family members, consultants—whoever can help. This will help keep your decisions objective and prevent you from going off the deep end.

Now set goals
At the Opportunities Meeting, you will identify opportunities that may have the potential to increase your sales and profits by 200% or more.

If you discover a low-risk, high-potential opportunity that requires urgent action, or if there is no reason not to act, why wait seven weeks until you have finished your plan? Go for it. But—don't let the pursuit divert you from finishing your plan.

The next chapter will help you solidify your opportunities by tying them to realistic goals.

Simple-minded approaches to sales forecasting for major customers can fatally undermine your plan. Reality-based sales forecasting is also simple—but not simple minded.

CHAPTER 3

SET GOALS

You have come up with the opportunities that will drive your company forward in the coming year. You may already be implementing one of them. Depending on where you are starting from, next year may mark a turn-around or set a record. Isn't planning great? And this is only the beginning. It just gets better.

The next step is to set goals. At the very least, you'll want to set (or review) goals that relate to the opportunities you've selected.

Why goals?

We are out to create a marketing and sales plan, not a marketing and sales wish. A plan requires goals. Without goals, it is impossible to evaluate the success of a plan, and therefore impossible to scientifically improve the plan.

Goals are measurable

For many people, the word "goal" brings to mind visions of sports. These can be useful pictures. To score in a sport, a definable event must take place. To win a race, a runner must cross the finish line ahead of all her competitors. To score a touchdown, the football must cross the plane of the goal line. If a football team starts a drive on its own 20-yard line, and needs a touchdown, the coach has to come up with a series of plays to move the ball exactly 80 yards. A plan designed to "move the ball up the field quite a ways" is far less likely to result in a win.

Sounds obvious, right? Yet, how many times have you seen a football team on third down call a play that's unlikely to produce the yardage necessary for a first down even if it works? The team is working on a wish, not a plan.

I've seen many equivalents in marketing and sales. One of the most common relates to advertising. Business owners often site "ineffective advertising" as a problem that plagues them. They tell me, "Nothing happens when we advertise." I ask, "What isn't happening? What were you hoping would happen?" Too often, blank faces reveal that the advertising campaign had no clear goals. The ads were supposed to carry the company "up the field quite a ways."

Another example of operating without defined goals is the "Que será será—Whatever will be will be" approach to sales. Management develops new opportunities, such as new products or services, or devises new marketing and sales tactics, and then says "Let's see what happens." But how can an opportunity or tactic be evaluated in the absence of goals? Is it worth pursuing? Will it be profitable? Is it better than another approach? Who knows? ¡Que será será!

Sales forecasts

Setting goals requires sales forecasting. We're going to talk about two methods of sales forecasting:

- Simple-minded
- Reality-based

You've probably figured out which one we prefer.

Simple-minded sales forecasting

There are several simple-minded approaches to sales forecasting.

- **Flat** Customer X bought $100,000 this year. Therefore Customer X will buy $100,000 next year.

- **Arithmetic projection** Customer X bought $50,000 last year and $100,000 this year. Therefore Customer X will buy $150,000 next year.

- **Geometric projection** Customer X bought $50,000 last year and $100,000 this year. Therefore Customer X will buy $200,000 next year.

- **Internally driven** Customer X bought $100,000 this year. Our management has called for a 15% increase in sales. Therefore Customer X will buy $115,000 next year.

If yours is a retail operation, substitute "Store X sold" for "Customer X bought."

Simple-minded approaches have three things in common: they are easy, they are not based in reality, and they do not require the participation of frontline sales people.

Why will Customer X buy the same amount next year as last year, or some fixed percentage thereof? How do we know that Customer X won't go out of business, or won't get an order five times bigger than any it's ever had, requiring five times more of what our company supplies? Maybe they'll drop the product line that requires what we supply, or get taken over by a company with allegiance to one of our competitors. Any one of a dozen other changes could affect our sales. Simple-minded approaches to sales forecasting for major customers can fatally undermine your marketing and sales plan.

Reality-based sales forecasting

Reality-based sales forecasting is also simple—but not simple minded. Here's how it works. A salesperson sits down with people from Customer X several months ahead of time, and asks this question, or some variation on it: "In the year that's coming up, how much of our product or service do you think you'll use?"

A good salesperson will already know things about Customer X that help create a meaningful dialog. "You're planning to launch a marketing campaign in a new area. How much more of our product do you estimate that orders resulting from that campaign will require?" "We've talked about how our new [whatever] will help your [whatever]. Do you have an estimate of how much you'll need?"

A good sales person will know how to motivate the customer to help with the forecast. "We need to make these estimates so that we can be ready to meet your needs without a hitch. We want you to give us the best estimate you can, because we are going to make plans based on these estimates. But we understand that these are estimates, not orders, and that things can change."

As you can see, reality-based forecasting involves frontline salespeople and asking questions of customers rather than making guesses based on previous numbers.

Getting buy-in from your salespeople

Salespeople tend to hate making forecasts, for some of the following reasons:

- They've been required to use simple-minded approaches, and they think it's time-wasting BS (baseless supposition).

- They've been asked to make forecasts for every customer, including lots of small customers whose numbers are relatively insignificant.

- They've been attacked for selling less than they forecast. Or for selling more!

- They don't understand how they will benefit from making forecasts.

You must get reality-based forecasts for your marketing and sales plan, so let's deal with each of these objections.

Simple-minded approaches If your company has used these in the past, explain why you are changing.

Forecasts for every customer A waste of time. Ask salespeople to make forecasts only for customers who account for 2% or more of their volume. Or to start with their biggest customer and work down until they've accounted for 80% of their volume (which as we all know may mean making forecasts for only 20% of their customers). For the smaller customers, use whatever form of simple-minded projection is most likely to be right. It won't make much difference anyway. In fact, whenever possible service the smallest accounts from the center rather than allow field salespeople to waste time calling on them.

Attacked for not meeting forecast Tell your salespeople that you want them to do the best they can at forecasting based on having a relationship with customers that allows them to ask meaningful questions. Explain that these forecasts will allow the company to do a better job of meeting customers' needs, and therefore will help salespeople do a better job and increase their earnings. Tell them you know that forecasts are estimates, and that if you or they could precisely predict the future, you'd be so rich you could forget about sales. Make it clear that company policy is that no one is to be blamed for a "wrong" estimate, and that you don't want salespeople to purposely make low estimates so they can "beat" them.

Benefits of forecasting Quantum physics revealed that you cannot measure a particle's mass or velocity without changing them. Likewise in business, to forecast sales is to positively influence the results. And forecasting helps eliminate surprises that can hurt the salesperson and the company, such as incorrectly assuming a big account will stay big, or being unable to fill an unexpected large order.

Forecasting by product

All products are not created equal

L&M Construction Chemicals makes Seal Hard™. Concrete floors treated with Seal Hard look better, wear longer and provide additional benefits to the owner of a building and to tenants. Seal Hard is a superior, even unique, product. When we developed L&M's marketing and sales plan, sales forecasts helped us realize that by focusing on Seal Hard, rather than treating it as just one of L&M's dozens of good products, we had the opportunity to drive L&M to new heights in sales volume and profit. Seal Hard became the link that pulled the chain for L&M.

The example from L&M Construction Chemicals shows that forecasting a customer's overall need for your company's products and services may not be adequate. When the participants in the Clinic realized the potential of Seal Hard to drive sales and profits, they asked the sales force to make separate forecasts for Seal Hard. To do that, salespeople had to focus customers' attention on the virtues of Seal Hard. Forecasting started the push around this particular product. When the forecasts confirmed that this was indeed a great opportunity, L&M developed the marketing and sales tactics to make that opportunity a reality.

Forecasting by month or quarter

Especially if the demand for your products or services is seasonal, forecasting total demand for the coming year may be insufficient to define opportunities and plan tactics. You may have to ask for a breakdown by quarter or even by month. This can be a good approach to forecasting even where demand is not seasonal. It can make the dialog with a customer more reality-based. And it makes it easier to detect when actual sales diverge from the forecast.

Forecasts from sales representatives or distributors

Everything we've said so far applies just as much to getting forecasts from your independent sales reps or distributors as from your own sales force. However, when people are not under your direct control, it may take some extra effort. You may have to sit down with them across their desk, or over lunch, and ask questions that elicit the forecast. Or visit key customers with them...whatever it takes. When your company's VP of sales, head of customer service, and other executives get off their...I mean out of their offices and into the field, their time is well spent. In addition to nailing down forecasts they will come back with all kinds of information that helps drive your plan.

You may have to use these hands-on and hand-holding techniques with your own salespeople as well, especially if they have not previously been won over to reality-based forecasting.

Reality-based retail forecasting

Whether your retail business sells from stores, by catalog or direct mail, by telephone marketing, over the Web, or all of the above, chances are that there is no individual customer that accounts for a significant percentage of sales. Therefore forecasting is of necessity based on projections from the numbers. But projections based on faulty assumptions can be just as fatal in retail as anyplace else. So what do you do?

Forecasting for stores

Your ability to forecast future sales at a store, restaurant, gas station, or other physical location is heavily dependent on the quality of your information about the past. Of course you know your sales for a particular day, week, or month. And presumably you also know what products were bought. But do you also have other critical information for your business, which might include

- Number of walk-ins
- Number of phone calls
- Average purchase
- Statistics about returns
- Effects of past promotional tactics on all of the above

For example, if you ran an ad, how many phone calls, walk-ins, and sales did it produce? If you gave your present customers an incentive to bring their friends, how many new customers resulted? In the grocery business, the effectiveness of advertising is typically tracked by coupon redemption. Often, you can plan your advertising so that a similar element of trackability is built in.

Hopefully you have all these good numbers from the past, but how do you project them into the future? Like any forecasting, it's not an exact science. You apply new conditions to the old numbers. Just as business-to-business enterprises project customer by customer, you project store by store, not across the board. Let's look at an example which approximates the multiple variables of real life. Sales at Store X grew 12% last year from the year before. You have reason to believe the growth is related to continuing prosperity in the area plus increasing knowledge of and satisfaction with your service and products. And you know from a survey you conducted that a large percentage of your potential customers still don't know about you; you have not saturated your market. Based just on this information, you project another 12% growth for the coming year.

You also know that your most effective tactic was radio advertising. A 1-month trial of an increase in the frequency of your radio spots increased radio-ad-related sales by 50%. So now you plan to double your radio advertising budget for the year, subject to modification if it doesn't work as expected. You run the numbers and estimate that doubling radio advertising will add another 16% to next year's sales.

But, a significant direct competitor is building a store three blocks away. The competitor will open for business in the middle of next year. When the same thing happened at Store Y last year, it cut into sales by 20%. Store Y is in a similar demographic area to Store X. So for the second half of the year, you project a 20% drop, or about 10% over the whole year. You also anticipate lower margins as pressure on prices increases.

Except—unlike the situation at Store Y, your marketing and sales plan includes tactics to avoid loss of sales to the new competitor. Specifically, you are rolling out a "frequent customer program" to give customers an incentive to be loyal. You have nothing to go on except articles you've read in trade journals that suggest that such programs have worked well for retailers of similar products, your gut feeling that your regular customers will like it, and positive reactions from a dozen customers you've informally polled. You guess that the frequent customer program will cut loss of customers to the new competitor in half, and also (through including the program in advertising) pull some sales you suspect you've been losing to a competitor in a mall 10 miles away and to mail order catalogs. Overall, you decide it will be a wash: the frequent customer program on an annual basis will nullify losses to the new competitor. You factor this number into your forecast, realizing it is a WAG (wild ass guess, a concept marketing has borrowed from zoology), which you will refine based on frequent monitoring.

You have arrived at a forecast by assigning reasonable numbers to all the important, relevant real-world events you can foresee. Will your forecast prove exactly correct? Unlikely. Will it generally be more accurate than a simple minded numerical projection? Yes. Is the process valuable? Absolutely. In this instance, thinking about potential loss of sales to a new competitor helped stimulate a tactic to limit the losses and bring in new customers.

At sea without a compass

The general manager of a consumer electronics company wanted to test direct mail for increasing sales at a company-owned outlet store. We developed a program which included giving away a TV with the purchase of a package of other products. When the mailing went out, instructions were given to store personnel to track calls, walk-ins, and sales. Unfortunately, no one from the home office visited the store the week the mailing went out to review the tracking discipline. The store staff did not understand the importance of tracking. The customers were in their faces; the need for tracking wasn't. Two weeks went by and headquarters asked for the tracking report, but nothing came in from the store, and nothing would. It was too late. For an entrepreneur, being nervous, calling the store, even driving out there and checking the log book twice a day does not qualify as overboard management. By being in their faces, you get results...if not popularity.

Forecasting for telemarketers, catalog and online sales

Whether you are selling from a Web site or a catalog, or by outbound telephone marketing, everything we've said about forecasting for stores applies. But you must adapt it to your medium. You measure calls or hits instead of walk-ins. You might use 5-week moving averages of hits or calls, adjusted seasonally if necessary. In many ways it's easier, because the data is recorded electronically, either by the customer in the case of on-line sales, or by the sales person in the case of inbound or outbound telephone marketing.

The challenge is to create a database that contains useful (and easily retrievable) information about customers, and where applicable, to train your telephone salespeople to elicit and enter that information. Then you start with the most appropriate form of numerical forecast, and modify it based on conditions you expect in the economy and in your marketplace.

Set goals for non-sales targets too

We always refer to a "marketing and sales plan" as opposed to the more common designation, "marketing plan." That's because we are convinced that marketing and sales go together like a horse and carriage, to quote the old song about love and marriage. Too often companies create marketing plans (when they create them at all) that are divorced from sales.

But—when we use the phrase "marketing and sales plan," we don't mean to create the impression that our planning should be restricted to activities normally thought of as directly related to sales. Everything that goes into creating your product or service has an impact on sales. Otherwise, why are you doing it? Issues that normally come under the heading of human resources, finance, production, or legal might at a given time be key marketing and sales questions for your company. If that's the case, it would be absurd for your marketing and sales plan to avoid them. By the same logic, it would be smart to involve people from the relevant departments in these areas of planning.

We'll go a step further. In this period when change is the only constant and successful companies are market-driven companies, we'll say that your plan should almost always include two, three, or four goals not directly related to sales. For example, goals related to the development of

- New products and services
- New strategic alliances
- New markets
- New production methods
- New sources of supply
- New sources of capital
- New (and/or better) human resources
- Better customer support
- More efficient internal communication

Human resource policy becomes marketing edge

Affiliated Resource Group consults on IBM AS/400s, mainframe computers used by large industrial, retail, and financial companies. The firm's competitive advantages include specializing only on AS/400s and having their own AS/400s on which to develop and test software. Based in Columbus, OH, Affiliated set out to become a national force in its niche. Obviously, their plan required marketing and sales tactics to sign up new clients. Equally important, they needed more consultants to do the work. Starting with 14 consultants, they wanted to reach 100 within a specified time period. They set interim goals: so many resumes in by this date, so many interviews by another date, so many hires by a later date. To maintain the firm's exacting quality and client service standards, the new consultants had to be experienced, high level people.

The Affiliated planners looked critically at their goals, and concluded that they could not meet their targets by using traditional approaches. That led them to rethink the whole strategy of employing consultants. In their industry employees are typically required to sign non-compete agreements, to prevent them from going to work for clients or setting up on their own and taking clients with them. Affiliated decided to dispense with non-competes. Instead, they'd retain consultants by offering the best training, compensation, and opportunities for advancement.

Affiliated told clients and potential clients of its new competitive advantage: having the best and brightest consultants, who stayed because they wanted to, not because they were bound by restrictive agreements. And, of course, many of the new high-level consultants brought clients with them.

What might have been thought of as a human resource and legal issue became a powerful element of Affiliated's successful marketing and sales plan.

It's critical to set numerical targets for non-sales as well as sales goals. If Affiliated Resource Group had contented itself with saying, "We need more consultants," they would not have succeeded in hiring enough high-level people to support the expansion of their client base. And they would certainly not have been driven to rethink the strategy of employment in their industry.

If R&D is an important part of your plan, you might have goals such as "Joe will talk to two salespeople (and/or customers) per week about what problems we might be able to help customers solve, and every two months he'll report to marketing on the ideas with the highest potential," "R&D will always be working on three new products, so that as one is dropped or goes into production, another is added," and "From among our best customers, every year we'll develop two as additional beta testers of our new products or services."

If you perform professional services and networking is an important tactic in your plan, you might have goals such as, "I'll have breakfast or lunch four times each week with potential clients or referral sources," "I'll help the people in my network by referring at least one genuine potential client a week to someone," and "By the end of a year, I will have developed three people in my network, each of whom understands the benefits of referring me and helps me land at least one important new client each year."

How to measure "soft" goals

Everyone agrees that sales can be measured, but how do you measure categories such as image, recognition, reputation, market acceptance, or goodwill?

You could invest an infinite amount of time, effort, and money (except that you don't have an infinite amount) in networking, writing and placing articles in trade publications, image advertising, PR, and your Web site. There are plenty of consultants out there who will be happy to help you. How do you know whether your investment is paying off or going down the drain? Or whether you're losing out to your competitors by not investing adequately in these areas?

Market research can be part of the answer. What did people in your target market think of your company, products, and services before, say, the PR campaign, and what do they think now?

But market research can be just another expense unless the results make a difference in what you do. If your PR campaign was designed to increase your name recognition and your association with the most advanced technology among a certain segment of your market, and the research proves that it did, and then you say, "OK, that's nice, it worked, now put that binder on the shelf over there," well, what was the point of the campaign in the first place?

If you had a tactic all ready to deploy, it would make more sense. Let's say the market research shows that name recognition, which was at 5% before the campaign, is now at 50%. Furthermore, of those who recognize the name, 80% associate it with advanced technology. You had already prepared camera-ready copy for a direct mail campaign with a special offer and with a benefit for visiting your Web site, and a telephone marketing campaign to follow up the direct mail. You say, "The campaign worked, let's continue it, get that art to the printer, and go ahead with the mailing [of course with a test mailing first] and the telephone follow-up."

Now you've linked a PR campaign to a tactic with directly measurable sales results. And it was a tactic that you had in mind right from the beginning. One of the reasons for doing the PR campaign was so that the letter and the phone calls would fall on receptive eyes and ears. And the market research was a sound investment because it led to a decision: if it had shown that the PR campaign hadn't worked, you would have abandoned it or made adjustments, and you would have held off on the investment in direct mail and telephone marketing.

Try to think of similar links and measurements for everything in your plan. Alandales, a men's clothing store in Culver City, CA, tracks its direct mail, for example, by including a coupon for a free tie with a purchase of so many dollars. Their radio ads, though, cannot end with "bring in this coupon." But Alandales can and does track the effect that radio ads have on the direct mail return rate. Over a period of years, they've developed accurate, comprehensive information on how radio ad frequency, content, station, show, and time enhance direct mail results. They've developed similar knowledge about links between other elements in their marketing and sales plan: print advertising, window displays, longer hours, in-store promotions. Years of accumulating and studying this data have increased the precision of their sales fore-casting and their ability to develop new and better tactics.

It's time to find problems

You've identified opportunities and set goals. Your plan is off to a great start. The problem solvers on your team have probably been gnashing their teeth and muttering, "Wait a minute. It's not that easy." They are right, and their moment of glory has arrived. In order to take full advantage of your opportunities and reach your goals, there are problems that must be identified and solved. The next chapter helps you do that. On to problems!

Problems come in four basic flavors: not enough money, time, human resources, information. But first you may have to tackle insufficient honesty and responsibility.

CHAPTER 4

IDENTIFY PROBLEMS

Remember that childhood game where you "Take a giant step"? You've taken two giant steps forward in developing your business: you've selected the most promising opportunities to pursue in the coming year, and you've attached well thought out goals to these opportunities.

Because of the creative and analytical approach you took, the opportunities you chose are based in reality. Winning the lottery isn't on your list. Your opportunities are not mere wishes. But nor are they slam dunks. Turning them from potential to actual will take work.

The first part of that work is to identify the problems that could prevent you from realizing each opportunity. Chapter 2 mapped out types of opportunities to make it easier for you to recognize yours. This chapter maps out types of problems and their potential solutions.

What if the problems are overwhelming?

Sometimes participants in Dr. Revenue Marketing & Sales Clinics ask why we wait until now to look for problems. Why spend time selecting an opportunity, and assigning goals to it, only to discover that the problems are so difficult that it would be unwise to pursue that opportunity?

If that happens, it's not a significant loss. You preserved your list of temporarily passed opportunities; you can select one to replace the opportunity you've reconsidered. Or you can decide to pursue one fewer opportunity, thus freeing up resources to devote to the others.

But it rarely happens. Why? The truth is, you have already begun to consider problems. You selected the best opportunities from among those on your list by balancing the reward of each opportunity against the risk involved. When you analyzed risk, you inevitably thought about problems and whether they could be resolved. And when you assigned goals to selected opportunities, you probably didn't come up with outrageously inflated numbers (although it happens to all of us on occasion), because you took into account the real-life obstacles to be overcome.

So far you've been operating with an awareness of problems, but they haven't been the main thing on your mind. That's good. Too often negative thinking prevents business people from formulating opportunities.

Now, though, you've reached the stage of the planning process where it is essential to focus your attention on problems. Be creative and dig for problems, just as you did to come up with your list of opportunities. A detailed examination of potential problems is a critical step in achieving or exceeding your goals. By anticipating obstacles, you avoid tripping over them. You walk around them, step over them, or push them out of the way.

Incentive system would have undermined plan

After we set a goal based on the opportunity to turn Lykes Meat Group around, we searched for problems that could prevent us from reaching that goal. In addition to relying on low price instead of consumer perceived value, Lykes salespeople were leaning heavily on "discretionary spending." They were dishing out dollars in advertising, promotions, free goods, and other forms of "street money" that salespeople in the meat industry use to bring supermarket buyers to yes. Why? Everyone at Lykes was compensated on volume, not profit! A complete, immediate overhaul of the incentive system was required to reach our goal.

Problems with problems

In many companies, raising a problem without a solution is frowned upon as negative thinking. That kind of corporate culture can lead to problems remaining unmentioned or even unsuspected until they emerge as full-blown disasters, like the iceberg looming in front of the Titanic. It's OK to search for problems without, for the moment, worrying about solutions. Team members should, however, relate problems specifically to opportunities and their attached goals. Generalized gripe sessions lower morale and actually conceal roadblocks. Say "Senior management doesn't approve things quickly enough" and you sound vague, helpless, and hopeless. Say "We cannot meet our goal if frontline salespeople continue to lose deals because they don't get specification and price change decisions within 24 hours" and you sound as though you are looking for a solution, even if you haven't found one yet.

By deferring solutions until the tactics meeting you give the team time to find all the key problems, rather than solving a minor problem while missing a major one. You also allow time to penetrate beyond appearance to the essence of the problem. For example, a problem might first appear in this form: "Our offshore competitors charge less." On further thought, you might define the problem differently: "We haven't done enough to show potential customers that our package of quality, service, support, availability, and reliability increases their bottom line." Another similar example—"Our salespeople don't spend enough time with our key customers to learn what they really need"—might become "Our salespeople have to do too much repetitive paperwork and spend too much time servicing Mom and Pop operations with huge demands for attention but tiny orders."

There's a pattern here. When we first encounter problems, they appear to be external. Our competitors charge less. There are only so many hours available. There's nothing much we can do about problems if we accept them as conditions of existence. We can't control our competitors' prices (at least not without creating a problem with the Justice Department). And we can't add hours to the day.

On further analysis, we generally find that the external appearance of the problem is not the whole story, or even the main part of the story. Things that we are doing—or not doing—contribute to the problem. As Pogo put it, "We have met the enemy, and they are us." This is bad. We can't justify failure by pinning the blame on others. Wait a minute. We don't want to justify failure; we're writing this plan because we intend to succeed. Therefore it's good to find that our problems are primarily things we're doing or not doing. It means they are within our power to solve.

Two problems that hide problems and prevent solutions

The problems of each company, in each industry, at each moment, are unique. Yet they come in four basic flavors:

- Not enough money
- Not enough time
- Not enough human resources
- Not enough information

To get to the "Big 4," however, may require tackling a prior set of problems:

- Insufficient honesty
- Insufficient responsibility

Insufficient honesty

Would you rather report to your colleagues on the completion of a successful deal, or on a sticky problem that is hurting your company and will continue to do so unless corrected?

Most of us would pick the successful deal. Yet dealing with the problem is undoubtedly of greater importance to the company's overall health.

If you are a 1-person outfit, the same principle applies. Who doesn't prefer to celebrate a success rather than analyze a mistake or weakness? Yet which is more important to our futures?

Let's illustrate this point with a stinker of a problem. Put yourself in the shoes of a VP of marketing and sales I know. The owner's son has been brought in as a district sales manager. Hiring family can produces fine results, but not, alas, in this instance. The owner is a great guy who, together with his wife, founded the company and built it into a multi-million dollar business. Their son, unfortunately, is a lazy, boorish jerk whose "qualifications" for his position include dropping out of three colleges. You, the VP, have been asked to "work with" Junior to "bring him along" and you've tried for eight months, during which the son has resisted your efforts and alienated salespeople and customers. You believe he has no desire to change, and you know his parents have a blind spot about him caused by wishful thinking.

Assuming that looking for another job is not a desirable option for you, do you

a) Muddle along?

b) Focus your attention on areas where you can accomplish something?

c) Work around Junior so that you are de facto doing his job and yours, to the detriment of both assignments and your personal life?

d) Confront the owner in a serious and thoughtful way about the problem?

You don't have to be a brilliant test taker to detect from the wording that I favor "d."

What if "d" doesn't work? The owner says it's not like you to give up so quickly, and urges you to "keep trying" and "give him more time." He concludes the discussion with "My wife really appreciates what you're doing for Junior." What do you do now?

Insufficient responsibility

Honesty didn't work. The owner insists on keeping Junior in a position where he sabotages your efforts.

So now you're entitled to select "a," "b," or "c" with a clear conscience. Right?

Or is that too easy? If you take your responsibility for sales seriously, is it still up to you to come up with a solution?

Essentially, you were asking the boss to fire his son, and you went in with no fallback position. Admirably honest, but lacking in tact and tactics. You wouldn't want your salespeople to call on a client with so little preparation.

How about suggesting to the owner that Junior be transferred or even promoted to your staff as "Special Projects Analyst" or "Senior Consultant" and given a series of research assignments (which you just happen to have written up, and which if carried out will help the company and if screwed up or neglected will cause no great harm)? If the boss accepts this as an ingenious way out for him, his wife, Junior, and you, excellent. If not, how about being ready with the suggestion that the new assignment take place in three months if, despite your efforts, there's still no improvement in Junior's work as district sales manager?

When managers face problems with honesty and responsibility, they can accomplish great things. Responsibility, as we have seen from this example, includes taking the human factors into consideration and planning for likely responses. It also includes accountability—doing what you agree to do, paying attention to the details—and discipline and consistency—not letting things slide, taking nothing for granted, checking up.

As we suggested in Chapter 1, the process of creating a marketing and sales plan should help instill these qualities in your team and make each team member more confident that the others will act with integrity: honestly and responsibly.

Reluctance to report results in brake failure

Reddi Brake had 99 stores that sold components to brake shops such as Midas and Big O. Their competitive advantage against larger suppliers such as Napa was fast delivery. They told their customers every order would arrive in 30 minutes or less. For the brake shop that meant more cars on the racks each day, and more profit.

As a consultant to management, I found that the company was built on a valid premise, but there was a corollary. No one warehouse should ever get too big, because it would become unable to deliver orders within the promised 30 minutes. As more customers signed up, territories had to be subdivided.

Warehouse managers were accordingly told to report on the percentage of orders filled in over 30 minutes. But they did not buy-in to consistently documenting late deliveries. They didn't want to report numbers that would result in their warehouses being divided. When management failed to solve that problem, the business started to decline because of late deliveries and it ended up being sold to a competitor.

The "Big 4" problems

Not enough money

It's great to have plenty of cash.

There can, however, be a down side. "Easy come, easy go" usually refers to spending with abandon on a personal level. The business equivalent is committing funds without careful analysis of the benefits, the risks, and the alternatives. I recommend that you scrutinize every significant spending decision as though you were short of cash, even if your checking account is fat.

What do you do if you don't have enough money to take advantage of an opportunity?

Sometimes, especially in large companies, the money is there, but not in your budget. If that's the case, the trick is knowing how to support a request for more funds.

The marketing people at K&M (now a division of Avery Dennison) wanted to offer rebates on their ring binders and related products. Senior management rejected the idea on the grounds that it would reduce margins too much. We then conducted market research which demonstrated that rebates would increase sales enough to justify the risk. Repeat business would be an additional dividend. We went back to management with those numbers, and they approved the rebate program.

Orchids Paper Products manufactures and distributes budget tissues, napkins, and paper towels. Orchids' president had an interesting approach to authorizing funds for co-op advertising, promotions, and displays to support the retail stores that sold Orchids' products. The expenditures were conditional on reaching certain levels of sales. For example, if Orchids sold 50,000 cases of a product in a particular area, and the operating margin was $1 a case, Orchids could spend $50,000 on marketing. (In areas Orchids targeted for growth, they'd spend their entire operating profit for a period of time.) When customers asked how much co-op advertising Orchids would do, the answer was, it depends on how much you order. Really, the stores had to pay for the advertising. Orchids is a $100 million company, but this is a great way for a small company to spend money it doesn't have. A company could even pay for the advertising with loans against its account receivables or factoring.

What if you see an opportunity in connection with a particular product or in a particular geographical area, but that product or area is not yet producing enough revenue to support the opportunity? If you are doing well with other products or in other areas, you can "borrow" money from those profit centers.

"Borrow" is a good way to look at it. Is this a sound way to invest your hard-earned money? Is there a rationale that suggests that it will work? Is the reward measurable, and big enough to warrant the risk? Here's another way to ask this question: Would you be better off plowing the money back into the field that produced it, which has already proven fertile? Presumably when you made your list of opportunities, you concluded that the new area could help your company in ways that justify the extra risk. Maybe reinvesting the profit where it came from would involve the greater risk, for example if that market is already saturated or the product is becoming obsolete.

Give us more money. We'll show you why.

Associates Purchasing, a Los Angeles-based distributor of office furniture, felt that a new line of chairs would add value for their customers. They saw an opportunity in doing a major promotion around the new chairs. The manufacturer had offered funds for co-op advertising. Associates Purchasing used their own money to create ads for their campaign, went to the manufacturer with comps of the ads and a written marketing and sales plan, and asked for more than the standard co-op allotment. Associates Purchasing showed the manufacturer a detailed program, including projected sales figures, and not just an idea. The manufacturer knew they were serious and committed, because they had invested in creating the ads (suppliers often can't even get retailers to spend offered co-op funds). Associates Purchasing also explained that the manufacturer would have the opportunity to teach its salespeople how to sell its other products along with the chairs. The manufacturer agreed to provide the additional funds, and was well rewarded, along with Associates Purchasing, when the campaign proved successful.

Years ago, Marcy Fitness developed the first $300 home weight station. At the time, the company did not have enough money to support the product with mass advertising. In the sporting goods industry, that's almost always fatal to getting a product into retail outlets. Driven by lack of an "easy come, easy go" solution, Marcy searched for opportunities. Its salespeople were body builders who understood the value of the product and could motivate and teach. They created an in-store demonstration program, went into stores, and sold the weight station to customers. Then they taught the retail salespeople how to do it. Sporting goods chains bought their product because, like Associates Purchasing, Marcy sold a program, not an idea.

Once you have the cash to throw at problems, keep your profit margins up by continuing to look for creative marketing and sales methods that don't rely solely on spending. The easiest solution is frequently not the best solution.

There are hundreds of ways for businesses with little cash to leverage their marketing expenditures. Jay Levinson, the author of *Guerrilla Marketing,* has created an empire out of supplying information on this subject. Methods of marketing with little or no money include support from suppliers, strategic alliances, self-directed PR, and networking. We'll discuss these and other tactics in Chapters 6 and 7. To get maximum mileage out of such tactics they must be solutions to clearly defined problems that stand in the way of achieving measurable goals assigned to particular opportunities. In other words, they must be part of your marketing and sales plan.

Realtors with self-inflicted lack of funds

A husband-and-wife team we know are the best residential real-estate brokers in their part of town. They've been in business for decades, experienced the ups and downs of the market, and know every property. Oper-ating out of a modest storefront, they provide superb service. To make sure a deal goes through, they'll make up for any lack of knowledge and diligence on the other side, often represented by an inexperienced agent employed by one of the well known, heavily advertised brokers. Most important, they have integrity. If clients want to make an offer, but it's not the right home for them, our friends will try to talk them out of it, even after investing months in showing them houses.

Clients who buy or sell a house through these brokers become customers for life, and provide referrals. But most people don't notice this small agency among the barrage of advertising and PR by the big outfits. Our friends frequently comment that they could grow their company by getting their story out, complete with the many testimonials that their satisfied clients would happily provide. But they never do it. Whenever they go so far as to get a proposal from an ad agency, for example, they just can't bring themselves to spend the money—even though they live frugally and have plenty of cash socked away.

The underlying truth about our realtor friends may be that deep down they don't want to get bigger. Fortunately, they can probably stay comfortably in their niche, especially as they will soon be ready to retire. But as the pace of economic change picks up, growth increasingly becomes a necessity for survival in most industries. If you want to grow—or have to grow—but can't bring yourself to invest accordingly, you have a serious internal conflict. If we were pitching a movie, we might say this is "where marketing meets psychology." What's the solution? Sit down, think it through, talk to whomever you have to talk to, and make a decision one way or the other. Resolve your doubts about your business by making a solid plan, then commit the money. Or get out of the business and do something you truly believe in.

In a variation on self-inflicted lack of funds, sometimes small business people, even though they are making a healthy profit, try to fund their marketing entirely by money made available by suppliers. Other things being equal, they lose out to competitors who understand the need to risk a percentage of their own profits in marketing. For one thing, the suppliers will catch on. Put yourself in their position for a moment. Would you want to partner with someone who pays his way or someone who is always looking for a free lunch? As we learn over and over again, there is no free lunch. If you don't believe in your own business enough to support it, who will?

Not enough time

Microsoft has $19 billion in cash. It would be hard to argue that the company doesn't have enough money to hire everybody necessary to carry out its mission. Yet among the thousands of Microsoft employees, I bet you would find it hard to find one who says there is enough time. I don't think I'd be exaggerating when I say that I've never met anyone in business who feels he or she has enough time.

This is encouraging. It means your competitors don't have enough time either. So why waste precious minutes complaining about a universal condition?

You and your associates have the same amount of time as everyone else. The point is to use it effectively. That's where your marketing and sales plan can be an enormous advantage—if you have one and if you follow it.

I knew a man who owned an office furniture business. For two years he tried to get his sales manager/marketing person to write a plan. The answer was always, "Not enough time." The owner didn't like that, but he never made it a make-or-break issue, so you'd have to say that to some extent he went along with it. In pop psych jargon, he was an "enabler." Too bad. The company went out of business. It was an unfortunate way for everyone to find themselves with time on their hands.

Create a no-excuse environment

There are many ways to use time efficiently. The first step is to create a "no-excuse environment." In this environment, people do not lightly agree to tasks knowing that they can blow them off by pleading "no-time"; and once they agree to tasks, people are expected to carry them out. At the very least, when a person realizes that there's been a miscalculation about the time and effort required to complete a task, he reports the problem to his associates rather than waiting for someone else to check up and hoping they don't.

A no-excuse environment is the first step in using time efficiently because it drives all the other steps. It forces people to look for the most effective ways of getting assignments done rather than excuses for not doing them.

Create routine

When you do something in business for the first time, it's difficult to make a profit. The startup costs are too great. Therefore, whenever your company initiates an activity, your goal should be to make it routine as quickly as possible. That requires additional time at the outset for planning, but once the routine is established, it is an enormous time saver. People spend time doing the work rather than endlessly thinking about how to do it, bumping into each other, and having to correct each other's mistakes. As we've mentioned, one of the principal benefits of writing your first marketing and sales plan is learning how to do the second one.

To save time, codify the obvious

Rick Rhoads & Associates is a business writing firm based in Los Angeles. They constantly elicit information from clients on which to base newsletters, Web site content, brochures, proposals, and direct-mail packages. To routinize their information gathering, the firm uses a list of questions, including "What are we selling?" "Who is the audience?" "What are the key benefits?" "What act of commitment are we trying to achieve?" "What contact information should be included?" and "Are the people who will answer the phone prepared?"

Sometimes the client will actually write the answers, sometimes the firm's writers will use the list as a guide during interviews, or as a checklist after a discussion to make sure that all the key points have been covered.

Rick and his associates have found that while the questions are obvious, without the list, it is remarkably easy to go off on tangents and omit critical information.

Create outlines and templates

In a fast changing marketing and sales environment, many routines cannot be absolutely cut and dry. You need flexibility to creatively take advantage of opportunities and adjust to problems. That's where outlines, templates, and checklists come in. If your marketing effort involves submitting written proposals to potential customers, it would be absurdly inefficient to start with a blank page each time. But it would be ineffective selling if the proposal did not demonstrate how you could meet the particular wants and needs of each client. Therefore, your proposal template should have standardized text ("boilerplate") as well as blanks to fill in, which in some cases may be whole paragraphs or even sections.

Boilerplate has a bad name because it is so often bland and boring. The reverse should be the case. You should leverage time by polishing text you use over and over again until it perfectly tells your customers the story of how they will benefit. Review your boilerplate periodically to adjust for changing circumstances.

Templates and outlines can be used similarly for preparing ads, sales letters, direct mail campaigns, telephone marketing scripts, and 101 other marketing and sales tools, and for reporting on sales calls and making sales forecasts. These templates keep you moving forward in a groove rather than wasting time on side trips. *Dr. Revenue's Marketing & Sales Check-Up* is a template for assembling information to write your marketing and sales plan.

Use checklists

I travel a lot. There is no easier way to waste time and kill your schedule than by arriving at your destination only to discover you are missing a key item. Instead of fulfilling your mission, you find yourself engaged in forays to stores and/or tense calls to your office, where your associates must interrupt their activities because of your mistake.

Years ago, I found a simple way to virtually eliminate this inefficiency. I created a "departure checklist" (now it's stored in my computer) which includes items I frequently bring—plane tickets, business cards, ties. It also has spaces to add special items I will need for a particular trip. As I pack I cross items off.

Develop checklists of this sort for any marketing and sales activity you and your associates perform on a regular basis, such as preparation for trade shows, catalogs, sales calls, and sales meetings.

No time for non-starters

One of the advantages of not having enough money to do everything you'd like to do is you can spend all your time on the few activities you are going to pursue. Sounds like a no-brainer, right? Not necessarily. Too often, the budget decision is made too late to avoid wasting time. For example, to prepare for a trade show six months away you figure out in detail what your participation will cost, including the exhibition fee, a new booth, air fares, hotel rooms, and mailings before and after. You have a series of meetings to hammer out the theme of your exhibit at the show, and to decide who will go and what they will do.

The deadline approaches for writing the check to reserve space. The manager responsible, who only now focuses on the question for the first time, says, "Last year we spent 60K on this show and got nothing out of it but flat feet. Let's put the money into our sales incentive program. That's really working." Whether or not that's the right decision, it was certainly made at the wrong time. Thousands of dollars in hours, days and lost opportunities could have been saved by making the decision earlier.

Develop others

You can't be cavalier about attending to the details of your job. But you squander your time when you become involved in the details of other people's jobs. Assuming that the people you manage are right for their jobs, the highest and best use of your time is to develop them, which means training them and supporting them, not doing their jobs for them. Invest time in developing others and the yield on your investment can be enormous. When a sales manager creates forecasts for her salespeople, she is doomed to forecasting for them year after year. Twenty salespeople, twenty forecasts. When she teaches the salespeople how to forecast for themselves, she frees up a significant block of time—every year. And the performance of her sales-people will improve, because she is showing them how to become self-managed sales professionals.

Too many hats spoil the growth

My client owned two businesses, and was compulsive about participating in every facet of both. It worked for awhile, because Jerry is a high energy, high stamina guy. But he was so successful at growing the companies that he turned into a bottleneck. By trying to take care of everything, he got to nothing in a timely fashion. The solution in this case was to turn over day-to-day operation of one of the companies to key employees, and give them a stake in the outcome.

Outsource

Your computers are wondrous; your graphics programs awesome. You can design ads and mailings in-house. But you know what? Professional graphic designers have the same or better hardware and software. More important, they have spent their lives learning how to do it and are geared up to do it efficiently. They've developed the kind of routine we discussed earlier. If you have the bucks, you are generally better off paying them to do what they do best, and saving time and energy for what you do best.

The same is true for writing copy, designing Web sites, taking photographs, producing audio or video tapes, conducting market research, and dozens of other marketing activities.

Two provisos:

- Some materials don't warrant investing a lot of time or money. Do them in house if you have somebody who is good and for whom it is routine.

- The more you or your employees know about copy writing, design, Web sites, and so on, the better you can manage your outside professionals, and ensure that they create tools that sell for you, rather than tools that may be beautiful and clever but miss the mark.

Outsourcing makes newsletter happen

Brett and Madelon Miles, the principals of Milestones, Inc., a performance management consulting firm, knew that a quarterly newsletter would help build their business. Each is an excellent writer, but the deadlines imposed by serving their clients made it impossible to focus on consistently publishing a newsletter that would reflect the quality of their work. They hired a business writing/design firm. The firm plans each issue with them, interviews their clients for the main story, and edits the "Coach's Clipboard," which provides useful tips for managers. The newsletter is always ready for mailing on schedule, has elicited a multitude of favorable comments, and has helped generate new clients. Milestones, Inc. leverages the newsletter by posting the articles on its Web site, www.milestonesinc.com.

Take advantage of technology

Whether you hire out or do it yourself, creative use of technology can save a lot of time. (If you don't yet use email to communicate internally and with suppliers and customers, don't wait another second.) Piel Luggage needed to get their catalog published and mailed, but some of the products were still in development. Rather than wait four weeks to photograph samples, Piel used digital technology to create images of the new products by modifying images of old products. For example, a newly designed buckle was digitally placed on an existing image of a purse.

The Piel Luggage story illustrates an important general point about saving time: think parallel rather than sequential. This takes consistent planning! Managers are often so stressed out that they can't sit down each day for five or ten minutes and think, "What should people be doing now so that when "X" is ready, "Y" and "Z" are also ready? By not planning in this fashion, a manager becomes a bottleneck rather than an expediter.

Help salespeople sell

The batter returns to the dugout, and says to his manager, "Sorry I struck out, but I was thinking about our equipment order, tomorrow's lineup, and my expense report, and I couldn't focus on the pitches."

Preposterous? In a speech at a major conference, Arthur Martinez, Chairman of Sears, described a study that showed that Sears retail salespeople were performing over 300 tasks, of which only 100 related directly to selling. Martinez said that eliminating non-selling tasks had been critical to Sears' turnaround.

How much of their time do your salespeople devote to selling? Can you help them increase the percentage? Would that leverage your time? Salespeople often do what's comfortable rather than what's necessary. At Hunter Douglas, a fabricator of window treatments, salespeople spent a lot of time delivering and updating sample books for their retailers, but relatively little time showing them how to sell more. I recommended that updating the books become a clerical function. Retailers would still receive this service, but salespeople would have more time to sell. We developed a sales manager seminar in which this recommendation, along with others, was presented by the company to its independent fabricators as a way to increase sales.

Salespeople shed "C" accounts

At Amdraft, a division of The Klingler Company, most salespeople found that fewer than 10 customers accounted for 40 to 60% of their business. Those were their "A" accounts. About 20 "B" accounts each contributed at least 2% of total business. Accounts that contributed less than 2% were designated as "C" accounts. Each salesperson had over 50 "C" accounts.

Salespeople were told that the time they spent on these accounts would be better spent servicing (and developing new business with) current A's and B's, and finding new A's and B's. C's had to be serviced from the center, by mail and telephone marketing. Salespeople were initially reluctant to give up their C accounts. They said that some C's could become B's. They were allowed to keep those accounts for up to six months. If by that time a C had not developed into a legitimate B, it was gone.

Few C's became B's, but most salespeople remained reluctant to stop calling on them. "It's easy for me stop there; I drive right past." The company insisted that the salespeople instead use the time to visit potential A and B accounts. At the end of a year, 40% of the C's had been lost, 60% had been successfully transferred to mail order and inside telemarketers. Total sales were up 35%: each salesperson had added at least one A account and three B accounts.

Make a marketing and sales calendar

You know the key events for the coming year: sales meetings, trade shows, promotions. Fill them all in on a calendar (or use project management software) and you can easily visualize what has to be done to prepare for each event. If that had been done for the trade show we talked about earlier in this chapter, the manager would have been aware that by deciding sooner not to participate, he could have saved employee time. The calendar can help prevent another wondrous waste of time: you suddenly realize you're behind in preparing for an event, and you rush around, causing a lot of sparks and friction, instead of handling things routinely. Chapter 8 goes into detail about creating a marketing and sales calendar.

Exercise discipline

You solemnly enter regular marketing meetings on your calendar. Everyone feels good. Those boxes on the calendar represent a commitment: this year we're going to work our plan, pull together, focus, not go off on tangents.

Then stuff happens. Everyone wrestles with their own problems. Meetings get postponed. Meetings get cancelled. Meetings happen but half of the people "can't make it."

In the name of "no time," the plan is abandoned: the biggest time wasting move of all.

Marketing and sales is always in season

Accounting firm Alder Green & Hasson set up a marketing meeting every Friday from 8AM to 9AM. An agenda was distributed in advance, and all partners and senior managers who were in town were required to attend. When this proposal was being discussed, one line of thought was to suspend the meetings during the tax season. The partners decided instead to reduce the meetings to 15" rather than endanger the plan by going three months without meetings.

Not enough human resources

This problem area has two related parts: enough people (to use a good old-fashioned word for "human resources") and the right people.

When another body is the only answer

Some opportunities require full-time, or almost full-time, attention, and despite clever efforts to save time, everyone may be too busy managing other parts of the operation. At that point, you just have to recognize that developing the opportunity will require another body. What if there's not enough money, or you're acting as if there were not enough money? Look for ways to make the new hire generate revenue quickly, and to reduce the risk if it doesn't work out.

Let's party and profit

The owners of Charlie Macs, a 2-unit sports bar in Seattle, observed that businesses sought them out for parties and special events. They knew they had an opportunity in that profitable market. But everyone was too busy with their retail operations to devote consistent time and attention. They hired a woman who was a proven self-starter and already had the right business relationships from her work selling trips on party boats. They paid her a reasonable salary plus significant incentives, guaranteed that she would have no other responsibilities, gave her a budget and the authority to make decisions within certain parameters, and made it clear that after a 6-month trial period the agreement would be terminated unless specific numerical goals were reached. She did a bang-up job, and Charlie Macs found itself with a new profit center that also generated retail business by exposing potential customers to their establishment.

No right salary for the wrong person

One sure way to have "not enough" human resources is to have the wrong human resources. There's a saying in purchasing that "There's no right price for the wrong product." The same is true in hiring.

We've seen variations of the following scenario dozens of times. A company needs a marketing manager for a new division. The division is not yet doing much business, so management figures they can only afford a quasi-clerical person. They say "Jane will grow into the job," even though Jane has no education or experience that suggests potential as a marketing manager. Jane, out of her depth, shows little initiative or imagination and requires constant direction from people who don't have the time to give it, to the frustration of all concerned. She draws high-salaried management people into the details of every project she starts. The company's accountant could demonstrate that the real price of hiring Jane (who was a perfectly good employee and is now demoralized) is double what it would have cost to pay a capable marketing manager. Worse, at the end of a year, the division is still languishing.

The moral of the story: You may not always get who you pay for, but you will almost certainly not get who you don't pay for.

People who tread water eventually sink

Here's another scenario we've seen too often. This one involves people who once filled their positions capably but have not kept up with changing circumstances. For example, there are regional sales managers who flourished in the days when relationships based on a glad hand, long lunches, and golf did the trick. Today, when the ability to help the customer make money is king, these managers absorb 80, 90, or 100K in salary, plus fringe benefits, despite having become useless.

What should the company do? Either reassign them to where they can be effective, retrain them if feasible, or let them go. That may involve giving them an early retirement offer, motivating them to leave by reducing their pay, or other tactics. Carrying dead weight is a drag on the bottom line, sabotages sales growth, and demoralizes other employees and even customers.

How should the company have avoided "developing" people into the wrong employees in the first place?

Develop people into the right employees. Invest in your employees by training them in new technologies, new techniques, new realities. There is a school of thought that says employees are highly mobile these days, so don't train them for your competitors. But to successfully compete for good employees requires rewarding them adequately, and the best employees think that personal development is critical to their long-term success. If you don't train them because you'll lose them, you'll lose them.

Reorganize the sales system. In these days of rapid change, chances are good that if your system has not undergone a major renovation in five years, it's obsolete. Analyze what has changed in your company, your industry, your customers, and your overall environment, and reorganize your human resources and sales processes accordingly. If you have a separate marketing department, similar changes may be required there as well. For example, five years ago you probably did not have a designated Webmaster; in most businesses today you should have one, either in-house or an outside vendor.

Know who you are hiring

Extreme cases of hiring "wrong people" can occur when you fail to conduct background checks. Hire a professional firm to do this because of the potential for disaster and liability if you make a mistake. One of my clients called his new controller's previous employer to thank her for releasing the man early. She replied, "I appreciate your calling, but he hasn't worked here for a year." My client decided dishonesty was not a good qualification for a controller and fired him. Another client was growing fast and needed a new salesperson right now. When the results of the background check arrived, the new man had already been working for a couple of weeks. Imagine the surprise when he turned out to be a convicted thief. Did I mention that my client was in the jewelry industry?

Network with precision

There's a good chance that part of your marketing and sales plan involves networking, an approach to developing business and resources that can work wonders. Networking with the wrong people can be almost as big a problem as employing the wrong people. Lots of people like to chat, like to keep busy by meeting you for breakfast, coffee, lunch, drinks, whatever. But they can't deliver for you, and they're not people you'd feel comfortable referring to a customer or associate. Sometimes you can tell right away; sometimes you can't. Here are three ways to find out who is for real:

1) Seek background validation from others whose judgement you know to be sound.

2) Seek the person's agreement to follow up on something, and see if they do it.

3) Make another appointment and see if the other person has devoted any thought or action to moving the discussion forward.

Avoid wrong customers too

Customers are not usually thought of as "human resources," although with occasional exceptions they are both human and resources. In our map of problems, it will be helpful to include customers.

"Be careful what you wish for, because it may come true," is a good precept to have in mind when seeking new customers, or when customers come seeking you. Often we are so intent on increasing sales that we forget that there is such a thing as a wrong customer. As a result, we create problems that did not have to happen.

Roy Chitwood, president of sales training company Max Sacks International and author of *World Class Selling,* says, "If the customer doesn't benefit from the sale, the sale should not take place." So the first kind of wrong customer to watch out for is someone who could be a great customer…for someone else. A customer for whom your product or service is not quite right. Sure, such customers may deceive themselves (or be deceived) into buying from you, to your immediate advantage. But sooner or later they will be coming to you with problems and/or telling potential customers to avoid doing business with you. In the long run, you'd be better off if they were informing everybody of the integrity you demonstrated by preventing them from making a mistake and by steering them toward the best solution.

Here are some other kinds of potentially wrong customers:

- too small
- too big
- too crazy
- not creditworthy
- litigation oriented
- sleazy
- location inappropriate for your operations

Sometimes a customer starts out as a right customer but becomes a wrong customer. This can happen when they change, you change, or both. When customers become wrong customers, you should be prepared to fire them. But it's not always simple. For one thing, it can be illegal just to tell someone you don't want to do business with them.

If you've grown and some customers are now too small for you, you might want to keep them on until you can arrange for them to leave as friends, by referring them to someone who can meet their needs. There may even be an opportunity for compensation here, but be careful: the goodwill could be more important. The ex-customers will have good things to say about you, and their new supplier may reciprocate by referring customers too large for them to you.

What about customers from hell? Usually you can get them to depart voluntarily by not responding to their inordinate demands for free service, price reductions, and other special consideration. The trick is to face up to the fact that the relationship is doomed before committing a lot of time, effort, money, and human resources to it.

Customer loses contact with reality

My client, a computer consulting firm, had a good customer that was a major part of its business. The relationship also involved referrals in both directions. It appeared to be a strategic partnership. Then one of the principals of the customer became full of himself. He forgot that business relationships must be mutually beneficial, and began to make untenable demands on my client. He wanted to return a 2-year-old piece of equipment for a full refund, and he did not want to pay my client for any of the work done to try to make it work. Unfortunately, the client had not billed for progress payments. At the same time, the customer tried to hire a key person my client had trained, developed, and made highly valuable, and who had signed an agreement not to unilaterally accept employment offers from customers. The consulting firm was even willing to let the employee go in return for reasonable compensation; the customer took the position that he could hire anyone he wanted to, without compensation. I advised my client to keep the valuable employee, fire the customer, and develop safeguards against landing in a similar situation.

Not enough information

Carl von Clausewitz coined the phrase "the fog of war" to describe the situation facing military commanders compelled to make life and death decisions in the face of uncertainty. He added that as the combat continues, the fog thickens and forms "a dark and menacing cloud out of which a bolt of lightning may strike at any time."

I don't know anyone in business who doesn't immediately see themselves in this picture.

That means your competitors have to make decisions with insufficient information too. It's like time. Nobody has enough, so why worry about it? Rather than become paralyzed by lack of information, recognize when a decision is required, pick a course of action, and pursue it.

When Clausewitz fought against Napoleon in the early 19th Century, it was often impossible to know in real time what was happening on the battlefield a few miles away. Clausewitz might be amazed to learn that the fog of war still applies to military problems, even though we can now sit in front of a television and watch combat anywhere in the world. He might be equally amazed to hear business people complaining about uncertainty when they are drowning in data far too voluminous to read: data on paper, on their company's computer system, and on the Internet.

Make information usable

"Not enough information" often really means "gobs of inaccessible information." I've worked with retailers who have sales receipts for ten years in transfer files in the basement. They agree that the best customer is someone they've already sold, but they have no way of using the receipts to get back to customers. When they finally send the receipts to a mailing house and have them construct a list, or when they call in someone to construct a database for more detail and flexibility, they are amazed at the power conferred on them by accessible information.

A good database opens myriad opportunities; it is not solely an IT issue, but very much a consideration in your marketing and sales plan. Think through what kinds of reports you might want to compile, and work with IT to construct or modify your database accordingly.

Anecdotes are dandy, data is better

The president of a detective agency told me that a lot of their business consisted of a certain type of work for a certain type of client. He related some colorful stories to illustrate their point. I asked, "How much business?" He said they couldn't be sure, because they didn't code that information. "Why not?" We went back and coded every case for the last two years by type of assignment and type of client. (The records were already searchable by fee, duration, investigator, and a number of other useful parameters.) Lo and behold, we discovered far fewer assignments of this nature than the agency expected. Numerical measurement rather than just anecdotal evidence provided a more solid basis for formulating opportunities.

Make information available

We've talked about overcoming lack of money, time, and human resources by creating self-managed marketing and sales professionals, business people with initiative, intelligence, and imagination. To function in this way requires access to information. Restricted information is a problem; widely circulated information is a solution. Sure, protect trade secrets and keep proprietary information away from your competitors. But the bigger danger is depriving your own people of the data they need to develop opportunities, set goals, and find and solve problems.

Say there are 50 CPAs in a division of an international accounting firm that focuses on midsize retail businesses. An accountant in San Diego is trying to land a fabric store in that city as a client. She goes into the firm's database and discovers that a fabric store in Milwaukee is a client, she reads up on what the firm has done for that store, then she calls the CPA in the Milwaukee office for additional firsthand information on the benefits the firm can provide. She now goes to the potential client with a powerful competitive advantage, and once she signs the client, she is well on her way to satisfying the client with exemplary service.

Your plan as a concise source of information

Al Masse, a turnaround specialist, made a profound point when he was a guest lecturer at my Fast Trac Class at USC. He said that once you've written a plan, it interacts with you all year, serving as your consultant. The information on which you've based your conclusions is there, all in one place, accessible and usable. And your conclusions themselves become your most important data. They keep you headed where you want to go, even if you are a 1-person organization with no one else to serve that function.

Solve the problems

Once you've identified the problems that might prevent you from reaching your goals, you are well on your way to solving them. The next chapters, about marketing and sales strategy and tactics, are entirely devoted to solutions.

Concept statements are not mission statements. A concept statement connects your company's competencies with its customers. It is the heart of your marketing and sales strategy.

CHAPTER 5

CREATE A STRATEGY

You're halfway through the planning process. You've put together your team, selected opportunities, set goals, and investigated problems. Now you're ready to solve the problems by planning appropriate tactics.

So why interrupt this seemingly logical sequence by devoting Week 5 to strategy? Or, as Clinic participants often ask, why didn't we start by figuring out our strategy rather than plunging directly into opportunities? And, in the context of a marketing and sales plan, what is a strategy anyway?

Here are short answers to these three questions, in reverse order:

3. A marketing and sales strategy links a company's competencies and its customers. This chapter will discuss that valuable tool in detail.

2. We didn't start with strategy, as marketing textbooks often recommend, because it can be too remote and abstract. Many a planning effort has started—and ended—with strategy. Opportunities, by contrast, pull you into planning with their immediacy and excitement.

1. By discussing strategy in Week 5, you have already identified opportunities, goals, and even problems that do link your key competencies to your present and potential customers.

You could skip strategy

As we've said, the two biggest mistakes are not writing a plan and not implementing a plan once you have written it.

If your whole plan consists of a few solid opportunities and tactics, and you pursue the tactics with discipline, that will be a big advance compared to working without a plan. It will put you ahead of most of your competition.

Adding a strategy can lead to an even bigger advance—but not if it gets in the way of writing and implementing a plan. If strategy bogs you down, consider putting it on hold. You're going to write a plan every year. Write, implement, and evaluate this year's plan, and you'll arrive at next year's planning session with clearer thoughts about your strategy.

Opportunities help you envision strategy

In Chapter 4, I mentioned that when you were thinking about opportunities and goals, inevitably you were already considering problems.

The same could be said for strategy. The competitive matrix highlights your company's strengths. You selected opportunities based on finding connections between your strengths and your ability to meet the needs of present and potential customers. Opportunities are truly the seeds of your marketing and sales plan: as you nurture them, they lead you toward goals, problems, strategy, and tactics.

Strategy is here and now, not pie in the sky

Talk about strategy and within minutes someone will use the phrase, "Five years down the road..." Planning is about looking ahead. But there has to be a connection between what you do today and where you intend to be in the future. Given the pace of change in business, you can influence what happens this year and next year far more than what happens in five years. The only thing certain about the 5-year outlook is that some significant factors are impossible to anticipate.

Mission implausible

Another phrase that tends to arise in a strategy discussion is "mission statement."

Please don't report me to the Business Correctness Police, but I think most mission statements are a crock. They put forward general values: the business equivalent of clean living, motherhood, and apple pie. But they say little or nothing to guide anybody in running the business. Therefore they are largely ignored. A consultant I know quipped that if you collected those plastic cubes in which companies display their mission statements and switched them around among all the lobbies, the only way anybody would know the difference would be from the logos.

Marketing and sales strategy vs. grand strategy

Let's say you are the VP for Marketing of a company that manufactures X-ray calibration instruments. Based in California, you sell to hospitals and X-ray service companies throughout the United States. Partly as a result of a sequence of excellent marketing and sales plans, your company's sales and profits have tripled over the past five years. Your marketing and sales strategy has centered around the simplicity, accuracy, and reliability of your hardware and software—qualities for which many customers are willing to pay a significant premium. You have developed strategic alliances with two major providers of medical malpractice insurance to lower their premiums to hospitals whose radiology departments use your equipment. You've also developed a strategic alliance with a German manufacturer to sell your instruments along with their X-ray machines. This alliance now represents one third of your sales, and is growing.

Senior management calls a meeting to announce that thanks to everybody's great work, the value of the company has risen dramatically, and the German X-ray manufacturer has made an offer for the company that they simply cannot refuse. Marketing and sales will be run by the German company's US headquarters in Minneapolis. They intend to market your product mainly by packaging it with their X-ray machines. California-based staff not involved in production or R&D will be terminated. HR will distribute the schedule of meetings it has set up to explain your severance package.

Your job just ended as a result of grand strategy. Grand strategy usually emanates from the financial sphere, and perhaps should more accurately be called "financial strategy." The decision to sell the company was based on the needs and desires of its owners, not of its customers.

While grand strategy differs from marketing and sales strategy, they are related. In our example,

- Your marketing and sales strategy helped create the value that made the deal possible, introduced the buyer to your owners, familiarized the buyer with the advantages of your instruments, and gave them experience in selling them.

- The German company saw a marketing and sales opportunity— a way to add value for its customers—by becoming the exclusive source of your instruments, and making them available mainly as a package deal with its X-ray machines.

Concept statements add value

Concept statements are not mission statements by another name. A concept statement connects your company's particular competencies with its particular customers. It is the heart of your marketing and sales strategy. It's only a paragraph or two. Read it every day, or at least once a week to stay focused on opportunities that lead toward your goals and avoid those that scatter your efforts.

I'm known as an in-the-trenches marketing and sales guy, but an article in, of all places, the *Harvard Business Review* contributed to my thinking about strategy. The article, which uses Ikea's unique approach to selling furniture as one of its main examples, is thought-provoking. Its first sentence is, "Strategy is the art of creating value." Richard Normann and Rafael Ramirez, the authors, write in that kind of direct style, so don't be put off by the academic tone of the title: "From Value Chain to Value Constellation: Designing Interactive Strategy." This 13-page article was published in the July-August 1993 issue of *HBR*, and you can order it online for $5.50 at www.hbsp.harvard.edu.

Concept statements are an endangered species. Few companies have them, fewer still revise them when necessary and use them as guides for their daily activities. To create a competitive advantage, write and regularly refer to a concept statement.

Examples of concept statements

At the zoo, you first look at an exotic animal, then read about it. So we'll display some concept statements, then discuss them. First, one that my Dad used years before anyone coined the term "concept statement." It was developed about four years after he started his business.

Haskell of Pittsburgh, Inc.

We manufacture and market budget-priced steel office furniture. We sell strictly through office furniture dealers. We produce catalogs, brochures, and price lists of the finest quality so that our manufacturers' representatives can provide our dealers' salespeople with the best possible tools to present Haskell Office Furniture to the end user, the business buyer.

Our products are of adequate quality and provide excellent price-value for the user. Our target user is a medium-sized or smaller business which needs good-looking, serviceable furniture at an attractive price. We are known as "the greatest value in office steel." We are 100% committed to supporting our reps and dealers with outstanding service and innovative sales programs.

The next concept statements are drafts submitted by students in my Fast Trac class at USC.

Visual Mix

Visual Mix is a design group that offers small to medium-sized businesses a powerful spectrum of technical and creative expertise in the area of print production. We provide strategic thinking for clients looking to position their services and/or products by corporate identity system design, newspaper and magazine advertising, and collateral design such as brochures, press kits, and newsletters. Our ability to organize and control a creative strategy from concept to completion results in a synergy between the communication media and the targeted audience. Our services are enhanced through the use of state-of-the-art technology which optimizes our ability to expand horizons and increase cost effectiveness. By the middle of 1999, our services will supplement the print medium with Web site design and development.

Dedication to meeting the needs of our clients has helped establish an exceptional reputation for unparalleled professional performance. Our commitment to quality, client service, and on-time delivery extends to every task we undertake, regardless of size, scope or budget. Visual Mix is "committed to creative excellence."

FIESTA TRAVEL & CRUISES/vacationstore.com

Fiesta Travel & Cruises is a family travel, vacation, and honeymoon planning service offering valuable free travel advice from experienced travel consultants. Our vacationstore.com Web site offers extensive information on destinations and travel products, allowing for online travel quotes. Our Web site also offers online Honeymoon Bridal Registry, as well as an Engaged Couple of the Month and Honeymoon Couple of the Month section. Our Family Travel section features a Quincenera-at-Sea planning guide and information about our group sailings. [Quincenaras, girls' 15th birthday celebrations, are big events in Hispanic communities.]

Our target market are members of the Baby-Boom and Baby-Buster generation seeking value-added service in vacation and honeymoon travel planning. Our travel packages are competitively priced; we offer rebates and discounts not ordinarily available to travelers. Our "Meet or Beat" policy guarantees travelers the best value for their vacation investment.

3-Oh!-5 Creative Advertising, Inc.

We are an experienced, fully-staffed and equipped advertising/post production agency specializing in entertainment marketing. We work for motion picture studios, record companies, television stations, and an expanding corporate client base to produce consumer trailers,theatrical trailers, trade trailers, television campaigns, electronic press kits, radio spots, music videos, and sales and training presentations.

We market our services by direct personal contact, through presentations, and by distributing demo reels. We have expanded our business development and marketing activities to include a Web site, banner ads, direct mailings, and coordinated promotional efforts.

We produce outstanding creative products, and are committed to delivering technically and esthetically complete versions from the start. All projects are developed and supervised start-to-finish by in-house creative, editing, finishing (audio and video), and graphics staff, which enables us to provide thematically coordinated, cost-effective campaigns. We are committed to meeting deadlines, providing exceptional client service at all hours of the day, and to meeting our clients' budgets. Our quality control standard is 100% accuracy, and we are known for flexibility, dependability, and personal service.

Effective concept statements

Once a good concept statement is written, it seems obvious. You think to yourself, "This is short and to the point. Someone probably sat down and wrote it in ten minutes."

Do not be deceived. It's easy for the reader because the writers worked hard and went through many revisions. That's why every member of your planning team should independently write a draft of your concept statement. Comparing drafts will help you eliminate these common errors:

- Too general (more like a mushy mission statement)
- Too broad (includes items not basic to connecting your competencies to your customers)
- Incomplete (omits key relationships between your competencies and your customers)

An effective concept statement defines who you are, what you do, and why customers pay you to do it. In other words, How do you add value? and, What is your position in the market place?

Analysis of a concept statement

To help develop your concept statement, let's examine the Haskell of Pittsburgh statement. First of all, its two paragraphs total only 112 words—short enough to serve as a daily reference guide. Now let's look at each sentence.

"We manufacture and market budget-priced steel office furniture." Clearly states exactly what our product is, including its price point.

"We sell strictly through office furniture dealers." Clearly states our distribution channel.

Note how much of our strategy is delineated after only these two short sentences. If someone identifies a great opportunity to acquire a manufacturer of wood office furniture, or someone else suggests that we open a Pittsburgh retail outlet, we immediately know that those opportunities contradict our strategy. I'm not saying that strategy can't change. Just that we can immediately separate moves that would have far-reaching (and possibly undesirable) consequences from moves that fit in with what we're doing already.

"We produce catalogs, brochures, and price lists of the finest quality so that our manufacturers' representatives can provide our dealers' salespeople with the best possible tools to present Haskell Office Furniture to the end user, the business buyer."

If this sentence doesn't tell our marketing department what to do, it's time to hire people who can read. We may manufacture budget furniture, but we create top-of-the-line marketing materials, designed to help reps show dealers' salespeople how to sell our benefits to end users. The concept statement shows the importance of the marketing materials to each link in our sales process: reps, dealers, business buyers. It does not have to spell out details such as having the materials ready on time; they are implied.

"Our products are of adequate quality and provide an excellent price-value for the user."

My Uncle Ed, who was a stickler for detail, was in charge of production. If he were still alive, he'd be galled by the description of our quality as "adequate," but the truth is the truth. The key for our customers—and therefore the driving force for our business—was the price/value ratio. Our customers did not want to pay a premium for the absolute best, nor did they want to "save money" by buying cheap office furniture that would soon look ramshackle, develop inoperable drawers, and so on. This one sentence in the Haskell of Pittsburgh concept statement guided every production decision of the company, from R&D to day-to-day questions on the factory floor.

"Our target user is a medium-sized or smaller business which needs good-looking, serviceable furniture at an attractive price."

Lest we forget, this sentence reminds us where our products are going to end up, and why. Our dealers sell our products to growing (that's why they need furniture) companies that don't have to put up a luxury front, but do have the budget to pay for furniture that looks good and works well if it's priced to provide value.

The sentence also helps us focus on real opportunities. If one of our salespeople comes in excited about having played golf with a buyer for a global advertising agency who is "really interested in our line," we're going to look at our concept statement and say, "You know, let's not invest a lot of time and energy in pursuing that lead. The buyer may have expressed interest, but when he analyzes our line in his office, he'll probably conclude it's not the best purchase for his company. And if for some reason he does want to order from us, we may want to refer him to one of our dealers rather than give in to the temptation to sell direct. Our strategy is to sell through our reps and dealers. We want to avoid undermining the long-term relationships we've built with them."

"We are known as 'the greatest value in office steel.'"

Our end users may never hear this phrase, which we use as the tag line in all our marketing materials, but our reps and dealers are familiar with this image of our company. They know we've earned the designation and intend to continue earning it. If we had to boil our concept statement down to six words, they would be "the greatest value in office steel."

"We are 100% committed to supporting our reps and dealers with outstanding service and innovative sales programs."

This sentence is another reminder that a chain is only as strong as its weakest link. We are connected to our end users by our reps and dealers. Therefore we must constantly support them with service, rewards, and incentives that are better than those offered by our competition. This sentence too is a clear guide to action. If our shipping department is tempted to say, "We've got two people out sick, too bad we can't get this order out on time," how does that square with our "100% commitment to supporting our reps and dealers"? As for marketing and sales, every year when we write our plan, we start by studying our concept statement. This sentence reminds us that the plan must include sales programs that excite our reps and dealers about selling Haskell furniture.

Write your concept statement

If it's helpful, use one of the concept statements above as a template for yours. Your concept statement should be short, precise, and include all key relationships between your competencies and your customers. If possible, your statement should contain a tag line that summarizes your value to your customers. For Dr. Revenue Marketing & Sales Clinic, I use "Good medicine for the 'top line.'" For his business writing firm, Rick Rhoads uses, "Writing that sells your products and services."

Develop your strategy

Your concept statement serves as the strategic guideline for your whole business. In addition, you may want to develop more detailed strategy.

What is the difference between strategy and tactics? Doctoral dissertations have probably been written on this question. It's more useful to make the plan and carry it out than to quibble about terminology, particularly in borderline cases. In real life, after all, categories tend to overlap. For our purposes, I suggest the following distinction: Strategy is the "what" and tactics are the "how."

To pursue its strategy, a Toshiba photocopy dealer wanted to be considered on every request for proposal within its territory that could be met by either of its two largest copiers, and it wanted that to happen within two years. Therefore the planning team had to develop tactics that would make their dealership a "household word" among businesses of a certain size within three states during that time period.

Professional Resource Screening (PRS), which is hired by employers to do background checks on potential employees, sells through a sales force organized by the industries they serve.

PRS wants to increase the value of its established customer base and simultaneously support a major expansion of its sales force. PRS reasons that employers who are hiring, and therefore need background checks, also want to get the most out of their growing numbers of employees, and can budget funds to accomplish that. In other words, PRS has come up with a unique way to define a market that can benefit from increasing employee productivity. That's the strategy, the "what."

PRS therefore makes an agreement with HHG, an HR consulting firm, to market and sell HHG's leading edge workforce productivity tools. That's the tactic, the "how."

Once PRS enter into this agreement with HHG, it becomes a strategy from the point of view of developing tactics—such as mailings, advertising campaigns, or PR—to carry it out.

PRS' goals are to become recognized in the industries it serves as a provider of these tools, to solidify its relationship with HHG by accounting for 25% or more of that firm's consulting revenue within two years, and to increase its own revenue by a stated percentage by selling, but not performing, consulting services.

In developing its marketing and sales tactics for the next several years, PRS will be guided by this particular strategy of adding workforce productivity tools to its line.

How does this strategy differ from an opportunity? In real life the categories overlap. But if the PRS concept statement defined its business as providing background checks, the PRS planning team might have looked only for opportunities to sell more background checks. The new strategy may prompt PRS to revise its concept statement along these lines: "We help growing companies hire the right employees, and get the most value from them."

Spread the word

For a marketing and sales strategy to be effective, everyone in your company must grasp it. This struck me forcefully when Anderson Desk developed a remarkably successful strategy that was almost destroyed by a plant manager. One of Anderson's competencies was its ability to schedule production so that whatever a customer needed, Anderson could almost always provide it that day. Anderson had developed a "just-in-time" system long before that buzzword existed. Dealers could sell Anderson desks to small businesses which today buy from office supply superstores. Once the competitive matrix revealed this strength, we emphasized it in collateral literature and discussions with dealers' salespeople. Dealers saw that they could meet the needs of their customers without carrying expensive and space consuming inventory. Anderson Desk developed a program around this capability that rewarded dealers for cumulative quantity purchases. The program was a huge success, with over 500 dealers participating.

But—the program caused a certain amount of chaos at the Anderson shipping dock, with dealers constantly sending trucks to pick up small orders. The plant manager established rules that required dealers to make appointments for taking deliveries. Business dropped 30% before senior management discovered what was happening and re-established the old system.

From strategy to tactics

You've created a strategy that will keep you focused on using your competencies to meet the needs of present and potential customers. Now, your team can get to work on applying that strategy by devising appropriate tactics, which is the subject of the next three chapters.

D ivide tactics into three categories: free, almost free, and worth it. Why not think first about the ones that require little or no cash?

CHAPTER 6

TACTICS: FREE

I f you're like me, you may have already developed and begun to implement one or more tactics, without waiting until your plan is complete. Good. It's better to increase sales and profits than to write about it.

You have reached a turning point in the planning process. In the past five weeks, you set the stage for action. You put your team together, decided what to act on (opportunities), and where to go (goals). You identified obstacles to overcome (problems) and adopted an overall approach to developing your business (strategy).

From here on, you'll decide exactly what to do in the coming year. In Week 6, you'll come up with a wide range of possible tactics. In Week 7, you'll select the ones you intend to use, refine them, and assign responsibility for implementing them. In Week 8, you'll place these tactics into a marketing and sales calendar and budget.

The calendar and budget are the final reality checks and spurs to action. They complete your planning process.

Congratulations on getting so close to the end, and having arrived at the action part of the plan.

Tactics galore

Marketing textbooks usually use the term "tactics" to refer to activities such as advertising, public relations, promotions, trade show participation, and branding.

I define tactics more broadly. Anything you do to take advantage of your opportunities, reach your goals, overcome your problems, and carry out your strategy is a tactic. For example, when accounting firm Alder Green & Hasson decided to hold a marketing meeting every week, even during tax season, that was a tactic. Nor do I isolate marketing from sales. When Lykes Meats changed the incentive system for its sales force to one that did not reward selling at a loss, that too was a tactic.

In this era of constantly evolving markets, companies, products, marketing methods, sales channels, and technology, there's an oft-quoted maxim: "If you're doing what you did before, chances are you won't get what you used to get." With few exceptions, companies must tweak old tactics and develop new ones. Tactics are your plan's meat and potatoes. They are the specific actions the sales and marketing departments (and often other parts of the company as well) take to achieve your goals.

The planning team uses the same approach to developing tactics as it did with opportunities. First, a brainstorming session to come up with a list of possibilities, including innovative approaches that reflect the unique nature of your company and its products and services. Second, a more analytical process to select the tactics, and the tactical mix, most likely to succeed within real-life budget and time constraints.

I urge you to begin by using your imagination. Next week you can be a censor—this week, anything goes.

Suppose your company sells vegetarian hotdogs through supermarkets. Your strength is that your product has done well in a number of supermarkets in upscale neighborhoods in New England. Your opportunity based on that strength is to roll out nationally in supermarkets with similar demographics. Your problem is that 6 out of 10 times, your product does not catch on fast enough for the supermarket to continue to give it space in the refrigerator bin. Your goal is to succeed 10 out of 10 times, which is realistic because you have proven that veggiedogs can sell. Management has authorized $2 million for advertising and PR. The assumption has been that you'll spend that on ads with coupons in the Sunday papers plus a PR effort to place feature stories about the product in the media. The PR campaign centers on the health value of the veggiedogs, and how they taste so much like traditional hotdogs that even kids love them.

At the first tactics meeting, the product manager says, "Everybody does ads and coupons. Why don't we build cars with bodies that look like a bunch of broccoli transforming itself into a hot dog? We park one of these cars in the parking lot near the door of a supermarket where we're launching our product. It's got the veggiedog name and logo on it. We hire someone to pass out a flyer with a coupon to everyone who stops to look at the car. And, of course, we'll notify the press, especially small local papers and cable channels. They can shoot video and stills of people gawking at the car, and we'll supply them with all that health/taste info. But the cars will be a hook for consumers and the media."

Now the other team members are gawking at the product manager. But this is the "Imagine Tactics Meeting," so instead of jumping all over her with objections, her idea gets written down along with the others.

Fast forward to Meeting 7, Refine Tactics. Everybody is assigned to come in with two tactics to recommend and plans for carrying them out. Sally, the product manager, has researched her idea and talked about it with key people in the company. Legal has told her that real cars with people driving them would involve prohibitive liability, but it's OK to mount a broccoli/hot dog on real tires and tow it at night from one supermarket to another. Sally realizes that a fake car could dramatically lower production cost. She gets ballpark figures from companies that design and fabricate these things, and it turns out the veggie hotdog fleet plus towing and personnel to distribute flyers would cost less than ad space. Sally sells the company's PR people on the idea. They suggest adding carrots as exhaust pipes, and placing a mini display of the veggiemobile in the supermarket next to the refrigerator case.

Sally develops a plan to build one car and test the idea at three supermarkets, against the results of standard advertising and PR at three similar supermarkets.

Sally's veggiemobile tactic may or may not be adopted at Meeting 7. It depends on how the team feels it stacks up against the other tactics envisioned in Meeting 6. But, along with the tactics favored by the other members, it has moved from a "crazy idea" to a detailed proposal, to be implemented, rejected, or put on hold. At the very least, Sally has helped us envision the process for developing, refining, and selecting tactics. Now let's describe a wide variety of tactics and how they can help you toward your goals.

I divide tactics into three broad areas:

• Free
• Almost-free
• Worth it

It's smart to consider them in that order. All tactics take time, energy, and focus, so why not think first about the ones that require little or no cash?

In this chapter, to stimulate your thinking about possible tactics for your company, we'll talk about 14 free tactics. In the next chapter, we'll discuss 11 almost-free tactics. Chapter 8 contains seven worth-it tactics. We're not suggesting you restrict your considerations to these tactics; we're just providing some food for thought.

Free tactics

Your plan

If tactics include anything you do to reach your goals, your plan is a tactic. The plan puts everything you need to keep you on your marketing and sales track in one place. If that one place is your desk, in your computer, or at some other location where you can constantly refer to it, your plan contributes structure, discipline, and organization to your efforts. You manage proactively rather than rushing around to put out fires or just performing day-to-day activities, which is the equivalent of sitting in the firehouse waiting for an alarm.

Your competitive matrix

The competitive matrix is part of your plan, but it's worth singling out. In fact, it's worth enlarging, and posting on the wall of your war room (or growth room or greenhouse), where your entire team can be frequently reminded of your strengths relative to your competition. If you have matrixes for direct and indirect competitors, post both of them.

Another use of your competitive matrix is to help you focus on an area where you are weak relative to your competition. Suppose you have a great product, but are known for poor customer service. Take steps to improve customer service, and then market that improvement.

Sales forecasting

Continue to involve salespeople in reviewing and revising sales forecasts throughout the year. This will keep you aware of new problems and new opportunities. If an important customer is decreasing its orders, why? Can something be done about it? If an important customer is increasing its orders, why? Is there a lesson that can be applied to other customers? Is a trend becoming discernible as to which products and services are selling above their forecasts and which below? Can that be translated into an opportunity?

Answering the phone

Are you confident that your company's phone is always answered effectively? A friend of mine is a real estate consultant. He charges $5,000 a day to help commercial real estate owners solve problems. My friend arrived in Houston to consult with the owner of a newly erected downtown office tower. It was during the oil bust. Like the other new construction the building was empty, begging for tenants. The owner picked up my friend at the airport in a Mercedes and took him to his private club for lunch, where they enjoyed excellent wine. Then they drove to the real estate office in the otherwise empty 20-story building. An attractive young woman sat at the receptionist's desk. As they walked in, she answered the phone: "Yeah?"

My friend joined the owner in his office. He said, "The opportunity in business is a window. It starts out this wide. [He held one hand at shoulder height, the other at mid-thigh.] Your window just went to here. [His hands went to chest level, about two inches apart.]"

If money is tight, before you answer the phone on the cheap, trade in the Mercedes, give up the private club, drink water, do whatever it takes to keep that window wide open. Does your telephone operator know the name of every important customer? How do you feel when you call a company you do a lot of business with and there's no recognition of that by the person who answers the phone? Maybe it's your accounting firm or your advertising agency. You pay them big bucks. You give the operator your name and ask for your party, and the operator asks, "May I tell her what it's in reference to?" as if you were a cold caller selling discount office supplies. How hard is it to train telephone operators to understand that their job is to represent your company? Why not give the operator a list, paper or electronic, of important customers and associates? Such a list next to every phone can help an employee who's working after hours know when special steps to help a customer are called for.

It's a pleasure when a live voice rather than a microchip answers the phone. But my pleasure quickly turns to pain if the person turns out to know less about what's going on than the chip. If I have to leave a message, give me voicemail any day. The chance for error is greatly reduced when there is no intermediary between my words and your ear.

Outgoing letters, faxes, and email

Are you confident that every fax that goes out of your office is typewritten? That every letter, fax, and email is in solid English that says what it's supposed to say? That each addresses only one subject, and that the subject is clearly identified? That each is sent to the right person? That if three people should receive a copy, it's sent to all three?

You may have employees who do not write English well, because it's their second language or for some other reason. Nevertheless, whatever it takes, do not allow written material to go out of your office with misspellings, typos, bad grammar, and illogical, murky statements. Some people think email is an excuse to slaughter the language. Your well-written, well-thought-out email will stand out all the more. Whatever the medium, I try to take a little more time, and be a little less rushed, to reduce errors and sharpen my messages. When appropriate, I have someone review them before they go out.

Sales force management and self management

Involving salespeople in forecasting is just one part of managing a sales force in such a way that they become self-managed sales professionals.

Ask yourself if your salespeople measure up to these nine attributes of self-managed professionals.

- Understand customers/clients and their needs. Document those needs for the entire firm's benefit.

- Understand your company's planning needs and fully contribute to the revenue-forecasting and planning procedures of the firm.

- Embrace technology and utilize it to maximize productivity and drive business development.

- Professionally network to build revenue and marketing opportunities for the firm.

- Prepare for all calls with a professional "Call Organizer" to make efficient use of the customer's and the salesperson's time.

- Report regularly in a systematic, professional manner as prescribed by the sales manager.

- Consistently plan new business development efforts to meet clear, quantified objectives.

- Understand the company's compensation program and aggressively strive to maximize personal income without sacrificing the company's profits.

- Participate in company activities and back-sell staff and management personnel to create a positive, productive attitude toward business development, marketing, and sales throughout the firm.

If your company is not yet nine for nine, what combination of reorganizing, hiring and firing, and training is necessary? Depending on your answer, aspects of this tactic could be bumped into the "almost free" or "worth it" category.

"Call Organizer" helps "schleppers" become sales professionals

The president of a $200-million apparel company vented his frustration, "Our salespeople don't sell, they schlep. They show hangers with dresses on them. If the customer likes a dress, they take the order."

We created a one day "Call Organizer" seminar for this company focused entirely on preparation for calls. This intense session resulted in sales managers requiring a new approach to the monthly market/trade shows. Salespeople are expected to have a Call Organizer for every one of their significant buyers, to enable them to professionally meet that buyer's needs. The Call Organizer has become the tool for directing all communication about an account.

In the Manufacturers' Rep environment we are leveraging the Call Organizer into a total sales force management system by automating the Call Organizer within software such as Act!. The owner/president of a Long Island, NY based Rep firm selling industrial tools and consumables has such a system in place. He says, "From my desk I can review every call for every line. When a manufacturer we represent wants to know what we are doing for them, I have the answers at my fingertips. This is a hell of a competitive edge."

Networking

You have to eat breakfast and lunch; it doesn't cost you a thing to build relationships with key people while doing it. The key word is "key." As we mentioned in connection with the problem of "not enough time," there are people who will be glad to spend time with you whom you can't help and who can't help you.

Approach networking with a get-rich-quick attitude, and you will quickly conclude networking doesn't work. It takes time to build confidence and trust. You should think at least as much about how you can help others as about how they can help you. But take the right approach to networking, and do it consistently with the right people, and it will be one of the best ways you can leverage your time. When a respected "influencer" believes in you, he or she can bring you an endless supply of new customers. The influencer earns the appreciation of the people whom you benefit. When you in turn refer capable, accountable people—people with integrity—to your customers and associates, they perceive you as adding value beyond the product or service you provide, and therefore want to continue to do business with you.

I'm a member of Professionals Network Group (PNG), an organization of 650 senior level professionals in California that has systematized this approach to building business. You can learn more about PNG and its emphasis on mutual accountability at www.png.org.

Not every person in your network has to be in a position to refer business. Your network is even more powerful when it includes resources who can help your customers, who can bring you important information, who can help you find the right suppliers, consultants, and employees, and who can listen objectively to your problems and help you resolve them.

Visibility is an important aspect of networking. You don't have to give yourself a brand name and wear a white coat, as I do, but you do want to be remembered. A stock broker I'm acquainted with is known as "the guy with the suspenders" because of the colorful suspenders he wears with his dark suits. Wear your badge with your name on it. Come to networking functions prepared to say something. Introduce the speaker. Sit next to somebody you don't know, and find out who they are and what they do.

As a manager, in addition to networking yourself, you can increase the power of networking for your company by helping your associates become good networkers. For example, networking should be a component of the plan of each of your self-managed sales professionals.

Finally, and in the long run perhaps most important, through networking you'll develop ties with a few people which turn into lasting friendships that transcend business.

Warranties

Your accountant might faint at seeing warranties in a list of free tactics. I never would have included warranties in this category until I consulted for Carpeteria, a chain of carpet stores. We were working with the franchisees, and the subject of warranties came up. One franchisee asked if I'd ever read a carpet manufacturer's warranty. I hadn't. "Well," he went on, "you couldn't stay awake long enough to read the whole thing. And you wouldn't live long enough to collect under it." He explained that it was really the retailer who was on the line. "Look. I'm the carpet store at the corner of Spruce and Goose. If I don't take care of my customers' problems, they're not my customers anymore, and neither are their sisters or their cousins or their aunts! So my warranty is 100%. You're happy, or I fix it."

That led us to create a warranty book. Go into a Carpeteria store today and you'll see that the book has seven different warranties. And on the back of the carpet samples, instead of just the name of the manufacturer, the most noticeable thing is the Carpeteria name, printed in a box with the warranties spelled out. If you don't like your carpet for any reason within 30 days, they'll take it back. Replace a carpet at a certain quality level after, say, six years and you get a pro-rated credit. If anything goes wrong with the installation for the entire life of your carpet, Carpeteria will make it right. And so on.

How can all these expensive things be free, or almost free? It would be more accurate to say that marketing them is free, because, as the franchisee explained, you have to do them anyway if you have a long-range attitude toward staying in business and growing your business. If you don't tell customers the value of your warranties, then they are just a cost from which you derive no marketing and sales value.

If you provide a good product or service, which is our underlying premise, then the great majority of your customers are satisfied. They have the peace of mind provided by your warranty, but they don't use it. Of course, if they cash in the prorated aspect of a warranty when they are buying again from you, the warranty is a profit generator, not a cost.

Can you give a warranty if you are in the service business? I do. It reads as follows: "Guaranteed! Hold a Dr. Revenue Marketing & Sales Clinic and within six months you will get increased sales equal to at least five times your investment—or your money back." The warranty helps land a lot of business. Entrepreneurs say, "If he's got the guts as a consultant to say he'll warrant his service, why not?" There is some equivalent guarantee of satisfaction that most people in professions and service industries can offer.

I feel comfortable offering this guarantee because making a plan releases energy that immediately impacts a company's revenue at least 5-10%, to say nothing of some of the spectacular successes that result. The guarantee did not cost me a dime in over 100 Clinics, but then it became "almost-free." I did a Clinic for a lawyer who had decided to enter the environmental assessment business, and felt he needed help from someone with marketing knowledge and experience. He was enthusiastic about the plan we developed on the Saturday of the Clinic, but by Monday he had concluded it wouldn't work, and that he had a better idea. I returned the fee and walked away.

Your logo
I know. Logos aren't free. But once you have a logo, using it properly is.

Let's back up a step. A logo is a key part of your corporate identity. That's a phrase consultants and graphic artists invented to mean that people will recognize you. Think Golden Arches, Swoosh, Apple. Often stylized initials do the trick: FedEx, UPS, AOL. Fortune 500 companies sometimes spend hundreds of thousands of dollars to develop logos. You don't have to do that, but you do need a good, recognizable, memorable logo that works for your customers. If you don't have one, get one. If you have a logo but it's outdated or ineffective, improve it.

Now, back to using your logo. If you've got it, flaunt it. Obviously, it's on all your "working papers": business cards, letterheads, memos, envelopes, mailing labels, folders. And of course it's on all your marketing materials: brochures, newsletters, 1-sheets, price sheets, catalogs, Web pages, advertisements, coupons. Everything. What about your checks? Your vehicles? Your product itself? Employees uniforms? The wall of your waiting room? Coffee mugs? Your welcome visitors sign? Your postage meter? For about $60, Pitney Bowes will put a slug in your postage meter that prints your logo (or a message if your logo is already on your envelope) on every letter that goes out.

Part of using your logo properly is using it on everything, as we've just described. The other part is keeping it consistent. Talk about free. This tactic actually saves money. You don't allow anyone to alter the logo beyond established guidelines for size. Nobody is allowed to act on the idea that, "In this flyer it would look better in green." After many years you might decide to change your logo to keep up with the evolution of your company and/or style. Make it a consistent, company-wide change. And, if possible, an evolution from the old logo rather than a radical departure.

Your Web site

Like logos, Web sites are far from free. But again, once you have one, you can publicize it for free. Include the URL on your business cards and letterheads, and in every piece of print advertising and collateral material you produce. Mention it in press releases and media appearances. And be sure to refresh your Web site by posting all those press releases and marketing materials you are preparing anyway.

Linking your Web site to others generally requires investing only time, not cash. Links to other relevant sites can make your site more valuable to your market, and therefore increase traffic from potential customers. Links from relevant sites with lots of visitors can obviously increase your traffic.

Most Web sites are starved for content. Post material and features on your site that are helpful to the people in your market, and over a period of time, with the right publicity, you will attract a following. If you produce content for your site, consider sharing it with related but non-competitive sites in return for links, banner ads, and other considerations. Kitco is a Canadian company that provides jewelers and dentists with precious metal refining services. Its Web site was one of the first to offer continuously updated spot prices on gold, silver, platinum, and palladium, an enticing service to bullion investors and traders as well as jewelers. Now you can go to many precious-metal related Web sites and you will see that they display spot prices supplied by Kitco, with links to Kitco's site. These links have attracted thousands of visitors to www.kitco.com, creating an opportunity for the company to develop a new profit center, selling bullion to investors.

Vendors as part of your sales force

At age 27 I was lucky enough to be hired to create Abbey Rents Furniture. Before that, I'd worked primarily in sales. Now, my job included buying. Suddenly I was popular among furniture salespeople in Los Angeles. Was it my boyish charm? Or was it the billion-dollar pockets of Consolidated Foods (now Sarah Lee), which owned Abbey Rents Furniture?

One day I went to lunch with a rep of a line of dinette furniture, an experienced sales pro. He noticed right away I was depressed. "What's the matter with you, John?" he asked. "I hate buying," I told him. "I love to sell. Now all day long I'm meeting with people who've heard that we're going to buy a lot of beds, or sofas, or posters. Many of them are clueless about our needs and don't take the trouble to ask for anything except an order."

"Time out," said the rep. "Don't you realize that buying is reverse selling?" It was a stunning revelation to me at that time. I changed my whole approach to vendors. The first thing I did was sell them on Abbey Rents Furniture. I wanted them to know why anybody who wanted to rent furniture for their apartment or house should come to

Abbey. Not only did this put unsalaried salespeople on the street for us, it also made these vendors better salespeople, because they started to understand our needs.

"Buying is reverse selling." Does you company consistently benefit from the power of this concept?

Let's say I'm sitting in your lobby waiting to sell you on my consulting services. Is there anybody there who will do anything to sell me on your company? Is there a receptionist who will ask if I'd like something to drink or to use the phone, a courtesy which I will appreciate, and who will also hand me a package of materials about your company and its people, products, and services? You already have all these materials. Will you take the trouble to put them in my hands? Or are you going to let me sit there, right in your lobby, and squander the opportunity to turn me into an unpaid part of your sales force?

When I meet with you, are you going to spend some time selling me on your company? Are you going to ask me questions about who my clients and business associates are, to see if some are part of your target market? Is everyone in your company who meets with potential consultants or suppliers trained to take this approach?

What about people you are already paying for products or services? How much business have they brought you? How many leads? Do they "get it"? Do they understand what you do, how you add value, and that they should play a role in helping you? Think about some of the professionals who provide services to you. Your accountant, lawyer, insurance broker, banker. What do they do the rest of the time? They work for other businesses and individuals, some of whom have needs your company could meet. Are they arranging introductions? Are they spreading the word within their firms, so that clients of their colleagues can learn about you? If they don't add value for your company beyond the narrow limits of the service they provide, how long should you keep them?

The owner of a computer networking firm told me that his banker had put herself on the line with the bank's loan committee in favor of a million-dollar loan. "If anyone had a personal interest in seeing my company succeed," added the owner, "it was this banker. Yet, until I sat down with her and pointed out that almost all of the businesses she finances could benefit from our services, she'd never given it a thought. Even when they were applying for credit to buy new computer systems!" The owner went on to say once the banker got the idea, she became a tiger, referring many potential clients. In the course of a year, four became customers. And the banker thanked the owner for enlightening her on how to better serve her other clients.

Employees as part of your sales force

You are paying vendors, but you are not getting full value from them unless they are helping you sell.

The same goes for your employees. If I ask you how many non-sales employees you have, the answer should be, "None." Whatever their principal assignment, every employee should be educated about the strengths of your company, and why it is in their interest to help your company grow. (If they can be given a personal incentive to help, so much the better.) It's 7 p.m. and the employee who runs your photocopy room is working late to finish a job. He answers the phone because he thinks it's a personal call. The caller is your biggest customer, with an urgent problem. Is the employee happy that he took the call, because now he can locate someone who can help solve the problem? Or does he regard it as an unfortunate interruption, tell the customer there is nothing he can do, and put him into the voicemail system?

To put the question another way, what have you trained him to do?

Owner participation in sales

People like to deal with the top dog. Rightly or wrongly, they feel that their concerns are more likely to be understood, appreciated, and responded to when they have the ear of an owner or senior manager. It doesn't cost a penny for an owner to help land a major deal. And is there anything more rewarding an owner could do with his or her time?

Like any tactic, this one can be misused. Top managers should not undermine their salespeople, and should not spend so much time selling that they neglect their other leadership responsibilities. But once a company reaches a certain size, the more typical error is for the owner to lose touch with customers rather than use his or her position to help drive sales.

Run great meetings

Your marketing and sales planning meetings have written agendas, distributed in advance. The agendas include the time to be devoted to each item.

Every meeting at your company should be conducted that way. The first time I had lunch with Rick Rhoads, my writing partner on this book, I brought a written agenda. Rick was amused; he said in all his years of having business lunches, no one had ever before arrived with a formal agenda.

The agenda got our relationship off to an efficient start. You're reading one result. Another result: Rick says that now when he meets with a client he brings a written agenda with him, and does his best to email or fax it in advance of the meeting. Rick says it shows the people he's meeting with that he respects their time—and his own.

In his 1999 book, *Business @ the Speed of Thought,* Bill Gates writes, "Good meetings are the result of good preparation. Meetings shouldn't be used primarily to present information. It's more efficient to use email so that people can analyze data beforehand and come into a meeting prepared to make recommendations and engage in meaningful debate."

Circulating an agenda in advance means at least one person in your company is thinking about how to have the kind of productive meeting Gates describes. As you've seen from your planning sessions, that leads to pre-meeting assignments to collect and distribute necessary data. Sometimes it leads to the realization that some people don't need to be at the meeting, or that the meeting should be postponed until additional information can be obtained and circulated, or even that the meeting is totally unnecessary. If time is money, not only is the tactic of having great meetings free, it actually saves money.

Add almost-free tactics

You're probably thinking about several free tactics your company could implement to reach its goals. The next chapter adds almost-free tactics to your arsenal.

Centuries of experience demonstrate that in sales, nothing is obvious. This is even more true when people are bombarded with tons of information per second.

CHAPTER 7

TACTICS: ALMOST-FREE

As you prepare for Meeting 6, Develop Tactics, you want to consider a wide range of possible tactics. Chapter 6 was devoted to free tactics. This chapter discusses a range of almost-free tactics.

Recruitment advertising

Recruitment advertising is not "almost free." But if you are doing it anyway, using it for marketing as well is almost free. Regardless of the position you're advertising to fill, simply spend for an extra column inch and put your logo in the ad. Think about it. I'm going through the classifieds because I'm unemployed or just looking. I see your logo. The first time, it hardly registers. But I see it over and over again, in every employment ad you run. After a while, I'm thinking, "These guys are always hiring people. They must be growing like crazy. They must be doing something right."

Of course, if you're planning to fire the plant manager, don't put your logo on the ad seeking a plant manager. Other than that, investing a few extra dollars to build awareness of your company is well worth it.

Merchandising
(and marketing your merchandising)

"Merchandising" can be spelled correctly with an "s" or a "z," and that's only the beginning of the confusion. People use the term to mean almost anything connected with selling a product. The dictionary says to merchandise is "to promote the sale of, as by advertising or display."

The key word is "sale." Merchandising is not image advertising, it's not an article in a trade publication, and it's not handing someone your business card. It's that extra something at or near the end of the sales process that excites potential customers and motivates them to buy...now. To put your product in the shopping cart. To sign the contract for your services.

Good merchandising is magic that makes objections to the sale disappear. Instead of magic wands, merchandisers use premiums, promotions, point-of-sale displays, shelf talkers, coupons, and contests. Instead of silk veils they use incentives for sales people, a.k.a. "spiffs" or "push money," to make products fly out of the store. Sometimes one beautiful tie or scarf will be presented over another because there's an extra 50 cents in it for the salesperson. These payments are "almost free" because you don't pay until after a sale takes place.

Merchandising intensifies buying incentive at the trade or consumer level. It creates competitive advantage. It can get you a better display, more shelf facings, increased customer advertising support. It can even bring professionals and other service providers more referrals from satisfied end users who know that there is a direct incentive for them, such as free services, a discount, or a commission. Even something as subtle as the clock not starting when they call for advice.

Merchandising to create in-store evangelists

Lykes bacon, ham, hot dogs, and cold cuts are sold in supermarkets in the Southeast. Lykes marketing and sales people, however, are rarely on those supermarket floors. You can't sell by remote control. Therefore we wanted supermarket meat department employees to enthusiastically recommend Lykes. But if you've never fried up Lykes bacon on a Sunday morning for you and your kids, how do you know whether to recommend it or not? We came up with a free coupon—for the people in the meat department. And we "sold" the store managers on the idea of giving space in the cooler to a company that would creatively support its product.

People in some professions tend to resist merchandising, on the grounds that a product or service should sell based on its merits. I've done a lot of business with accountants and engineers. Why, they often ask, is it necessary to add that little extra push to make the sale, when the benefits of what they do are so obvious? The answer to that logical question is that logic is not history. Centuries of experience demonstrate that in the world of sales, nothing is obvious. This is even more so today, when people are bombarded with tons of information per second, and may not even focus on a product or service long enough to grasp what it will do for them.

You can market your merchandising. I worked with Asics Tiger Corporation at a time when they were recovering from production difficulties. Retailers said there was no point in ordering Asics athletic shoes and apparel because the company wouldn't be able to deliver. To demonstrate that they were serious, Asics created new point-of-sale displays, hang tags, local advertising campaigns, and other merchandising tools. But Asics did not stop there. They realized that their commitment to building market share would not be "obvious." To get retailers to understand all that they had going for them, the company published a brochure on each of their merchandising tools. The unstated message—and it was often stated by the Asics salespeople—was, "Do you think we'd go to the trouble and expense of developing all this stuff if we weren't going to deliver product?" The retailers ordered, because they became convinced that Asics Tiger would deliver product and help them sell it.

Planning promotions

Suppose you are in an industry that is heavily dependent on key moments in the year, such as Christmas, Valentine's Day, Father's Day, or Graduation. You devise a promotion for, say, Father's Day. You take it to a major retailer, and their people are blown away. They say, "Wow, this is great." Then they add, "Too bad you didn't come in with this three weeks ago. That's when Company X showed us their Father's Day promotion, and we signed up last Monday. We like yours better, but we're committed, and we can't do both."

You can use your marketing and sales plan to make sure that you get in first rather than at the last minute. Depending on the industry you are in, you might sit down with your retailers (or distributors, reps, catalog or Internet sellers) and discuss your promotion plans for the whole coming year. You want them to commit, so you have to be organized, with a concept, a calendar, a budget. But you don't have to have every detail in place, particularly if you are talking about promotions 6-12 months out. In fact, you can turn that into an advantage—flexibility. A retailer, an important customer, may say, "I like your basic approach, but why don't we do it a little differently?" If it makes sense, you reply, "Sure, great idea." Make the retailer your partner in planning the promotion. With modern technology it's easy and cost effective to modify promo materials for major customers.

Promotion with your own product

Consultant pays for referrals with deferred time off

A Macintosh consultant we know used to give you five hours of his time for free if you brought him a new client. At $50/hour, that was a $250 value to the recipient. But it was "almost free" for the consultant. At a time when he needed to expand his client base, his cost was time, which he had, rather than cash, which he didn't. He gave away evenings and weekends to build his business. Now this consultant is so busy that he refers new clients to other consultants. And he charges $100/hour.

Tropitone makes luxury outdoor furniture. When they hired me to develop a marketing plan, they had advanced from $27 million to $20 million in sales. (That's not a typo. I just wanted to see if you were reading carefully.) They had gone to 100% secured financing, and were in serious trouble. Their VP for marketing and sales said, "John, "If we don't hit a home run at the Casual Show in September, we're out of business."

It was already July. We brainstormed about opportunities. The big, fancy seat cushions caught my eye. "Does anybody have a concern that they might deteriorate, out in the weather 12 months a year?" The VP said sure. "What if we tell anybody who buys a table and four chairs from us that any time during their ownership of that furniture, they can have a replacement set of cushions free?"

The VP said that would be great, because their retailers sold Tropitone and another, very similar luxury brand, and this would give Tropitone a significant competitive advantage. But, the VP said, "They'd never let you do that." "They" were the corporate finance people, the bean counters.

I went to the CFO and inquired about the cost of a cushion, direct material and direct labor only. He said $8. Then I asked, "If we could take sales from $20 to $30 million in one year by offering a 5% discount, would you allow that?" He said yes. Actually, he said, "I'd kiss you on both cheeks." So I showed him that $32 for four cushions was a hair over 5% of $600, the average wholesale cost of a Tropitone table and four chairs. And, of course, not everybody would take advantage of the offer.

Then the CFO added value to our marketing concept. "You don't need to give away the cushions during the first year," he said. "It's not very likely anything's going to happen. That gives us the opportunity to build up a reserve to fund the program."

We didn't just say you can have free cushions with a set. We developed a whole merchandising program built around the free cushions. To be eligible, you had to join "Club Tropitone." In the first year, sales increased 50%, from $20 million to $30 million. Retailers wanted to order $35 million worth of furniture, but Tropitone could not ramp up production fast enough.

Tropitone used a maximum of $32 worth of its own product to support a profitable sale that had already taken place. The perceived value to the end user was far greater than $32. If Tropitone had instead reduced its price 5%, they would have had to take the cost at the time of sale to the retailer, rather than at least a year after the sale to the end user or, in some cases, never. Furthermore, if retailers passed along the price reduction, it might have created the impression in the minds of luxury furniture buyers that Tropitone furniture was lower in quality relative to its main competitor.

Promoting new products

Let's look at a new product I'm launching that sells for $100 at the trade level and has a 40% gross profit, or $40 per unit. What is the most I should spend on promotion? Stop for a minute and think through your response before turning the page. You'll get more out of this exercise if you do.

When I ask this question at seminars, I get a wide range of answers. $20 is a popular response, because that still leaves a healthy $20 profit.

I usually say, "$20. I agree. Or maybe $30 or $40. Or, even, in some cases, $50, $60, or $70." Then I ask, "Am I an idiot if I'm willing to lose $30 a unit?"

I want the product placed. If it's not placed, every penny I've spent on developing it is lost. I promote the product to buy market share. I obviously can't spend $40 or more forever. But what if the numbers show that buying market share now will pay off in greatly expanded sales later?

For example, if I sell 10,000 units the first month, my gross profit is 10,000 x $40, or $400,000. Suppose I put the entire $400,000 into promotion. In the second month I sell 20,000 units, for a gross profit of $800,000, which I also totally invest in promotion. And I double the next month, and put in the entire $1.6 million. My plan is of course to reduce the amount at a predetermined rate. For awhile, though, I might even increase the promotion investment per unit, because as volume ramps up, the unit cost of production will decrease. It might decrease dramatically if we reach volumes that allow us to change to a different kind of mold or process, or move production offshore.

Some entrepreneurs and many financial people believe that every product must start paying for itself from the first sale. I look at it differently. Before we had this product, it produced zero gross profit. In fact, its R&D costs represented a drain on profits. Now, it is producing revenue that we didn't have before. So what's wrong with investing that revenue to buy market share? Sometimes, with the right product at the right time, by being aggressive from the launch, we can knock a competitor out, or prevent a potential competitor from entering the market.

If you're a marketing person in a relatively large organization, you've got to show top management that in all likelihood the financial statement won't be hurt by investing the gross profit from the new product in promotion during the first 12 months. In most cases, the new product just won't be important enough to the whole picture that quickly. Later, when the product becomes more significant in overall sales, is the time to divert some of the profit into the company's general revenue stream.

Speeding new products and services to market

New products and services are the lifeblood of any company. Every time you're late introducing a new product, you give away profit. But some companies are unable to roll out new products on time or at all. The "D" part of R&D shows up as a weakness on their competitive matrix. There is a solution. Bite the bullet and outsource development of the product. Many companies develop new products for other companies. It's their only business. They have to be good at it to stay in business.

You have to pay for their services, in the form of cash, royalties, or both. But every penny you invest in an in-house development program that doesn't work at all is totally wasted. If the new product comes in late, you've lost at least incremental profits and possibly competitive advantage you can never recover. So if you're not good at developing new products, the real high cost is for the seemingly less expensive in-house alternative, which also diverts your people away from concentrating on what they do best.

In the service business, new "products" are equally essential. You have to repackage yourself periodically. People get bored and tend not to hear you unless you present yourself in a new, exciting way. Even if it's mainly the same old stuff, it's got to have a new twist, or relate to something new in the marketplace. For many years, I marketed myself as a marketing and sales consultant. Among other things, I went into a company and helped them write a marketing and sales plan. Then I developed the "Dr. Revenue Marketing and Sales Clinic," to "productize" my services. Today, 50% of my business is in Clinics, up from 10% two years ago.

New service moves product

Associates Purchasing sells new and used office furniture. Businesses move, expand, contract, and do all sorts of things for which they need help with their layout and furnishings. Seeing that as an opportunity, we developed a package of move-management services which gave us the opportunity to present a new "product" to Associates' customers and new customers. It also gave us the opportunity to sell furniture which was easy to reconfigure and move.

Press kit

Virtually every business should have a press kit. If your budget is too small to support printing customized 2-pocket folders (known in the trade as "Duo-Tang" folders), just buy stock folders from an office supply store or catalog, and print pressure-sensitive ("peel-off") labels with your company name and logo to put on the cover. Now you have the outside of your kit.

What do you put inside? Pick up some press kits from other companies as models. Put in a "backgrounder" about your company. Depending on your skills, time, and budget, write it in-house or hire an outside pro. The backgrounder lets people know what you do, why you're good at it, who your key people are, and some of your history. You might include product sheets or a catalog. Then, as new developments occur—new products or services, strategic alliances, new hires or promotions of present employees—write press releases about them and include them in the kit. As the kit grows, remove outdated material.

Write your backgrounders and press releases in an objective journalistic style, so that people feel they are reading a story about your company, not a sales brochure.

When stories by or about you are published, purchase or make copies and include them in the kit. Publication of your words magically establishes you as an authority.

How do you use your press kit?

You give it to journalists who want to write about you, or who you want to write about you.

You give it to visitors to help sell them on your company.

You give it to candidates for jobs. Let's say you really want a top young engineer. She just graduated from MIT. You've offered a lot of money, but so have other companies. You help sell your company by handing her your press package. She reads it, shares it with her parents and friends. The press kit is part of your competitive advantage.

I suggest you give a press kit to every employee as well. Even if there are 600 of them, it's worth spending a couple of dollars on each one, and then including them in distribution of press releases as they come out (especially if you can do it by email, which is essentially free). Earlier we said every employee, regardless of assignment, should be part of your sales force. That means you have to sell them and keep selling them on your company. Your employees are already the first to know about anything negative. Why should they be the last to know about positive developments?

When you feature employees in your press releases, be sure to distribute them to their high school publications, their college and graduate school alumni publications, their hometown newspapers, and the newspapers where they presently live. This is a great way to get free publicity for your company and build employee morale.

Public relations

If you have the budget to hire a capable PR firm, it could be a good investment. We'll go into that in the next chapter, about tactics that cost money but are "worth it."

If you're doing your own PR, you already have the first ingredient: your press kit. The second ingredient is to cultivate contacts in the media appropriate to your business. Get to know them. Keep in front of them with newsworthy events or analysis, not sales material. Ask them about their needs and deadlines, and respect their answers. Help them (and people in your network) by calling their attention to newsworthy items and trends not related to your company.

If you advertise in a publication, are you more likely to get positive coverage in its news columns? In the trade press, absolutely. Some openly acknowledge favoring advertisers; the others just do it. In the mass media, not unless you are General Motors, WalMart, or Microsoft, in which case they are covering you anyway.

Remember those non-sales goals, back in Chapter 3? If one of your goals is "more publicity," that's too soft and doesn't lead to specific problems or tactics. Set a goal such as getting an article about your company in a specific publication within the year, and you are on your way. Let's say the problem is that the writer you need to cultivate works out of the publication's headquarters in Chicago, and you are in Dallas. You create tactics to solve the problem. Perhaps you develop an email relationship and you take him out to lunch or dinner when you are in Chicago for a sales call or to visit your Aunt Irma.

Trade shows

Participating in a trade show belongs among the "worth it" tactics. Here we'll talk about some tactics that help you get the most out of your participation, and cost little or nothing. In fact, they can save you big bucks.

The first tactic starts with a file folder. When you're at the trade show, whether as an exhibitor or attendee, make notes at the end of each day about sales, leads, contacts, information you've learned, and anything else that's relevant to determining the cost-effectiveness of your participation in the show and/or how you could be better prepared for that show next year. Get a report from everyone in your company who is at the show. Put all this material in the folder.

Back at your office, file the folder so you can find it when the time comes to decide whether to participate, and to what degree, in that show next year. If the information suggests that the show didn't—and won't—work for you, don't go. You just saved your company thousands of dollars to invest in marketing that works. If the information suggests that the show is good for you, use it to figure out how to "reinforce success." How about some mailings before and after the show? Appointments set beforehand? An improved booth? Special promotions? Now that you're writing a marketing and sales plan, you can set goals for the show and include actions months before the show and right after the show to maximize return on your investment.

Another almost-free trade show tactic involves your press kit, and those of your competitors and potential suppliers, vendors, or strategic allies. Ask the show managers how many reporters will be covering the event. "Well, last year there were 28." So you bring 35 press kits, in addition to those you'll need at your booth. You take them to the press room rather than just hand them to the show staff. In the press room are piles of press kits. Pick up one from each of your competitors and any others of interest to you. Take the material home and read it and you will find a gold mine of data on your competition, your industry, your markets. It will stimulate a lot of thought about what your company should and shouldn't do.

Of course you'll give your press kit to any reporter who expresses an interest in your company. Be sure to get the reporter's card, and to follow up, especially when you have additional relevant information. For example, the reporter was interested in a new product you were exhibiting, and the new information is that a Fortune 500 company has ordered the product, or that two key retailers agreed to carry it, or it's available in seven new colors.

Surveys

You can get valuable information by surveying your customers or your salespeople (or your retailers' salespeople). What makes it valuable? Using the information to help you make a decision. Therefore before you decide to conduct a survey, know what you will do if the answers come out this way, and what you will do if the answers come out that way. Don't put a red flag in front of good customers or salespeople by soliciting their opinions and then ignoring them. Do follow up by thanking the respondents and telling them what the results were and what you are doing about it.

Don't abuse people's time by overdoing surveys. One or two a year to the same group of people is plenty. And don't survey with a 40-page questionnaire. Keep it short and simple. This is especially critical if you are going to do the survey yourself. If you can outsource a survey to competent professionals, do it. Surveys can produce worthless data unless the questions are carefully framed and the survey is conducted in a way that does not skew the results. Even if you can't afford to entirely outsource the survey, it's smart to hire a competent professional to review your questions and methodology.

Customer partnerships

You may have a product or service where, in a certain market niche or a certain geographic area, you can only have one customer. When I was in the school furniture business, I could have only one per state, because they required exclusives. So I had to bet on the horse that I thought would win. Sometimes I had to bet on the horse that would carry me even if I thought another horse was better. That might put me in a position to change the following year. Not all partnerships are forever.

If you develop software for business use, you probably need partnerships with companies that beta test your software, in return for free or discounted use of the final version. It's important to pick companies that can give you useful feedback—and useful referrals.

Partnering is free or almost free in terms of money, but it's a serious commitment in terms of time, reputation, and performance. Think carefully before entering into a partnership, especially an exclusive one. Check out the potential partner, then test the partner by entering into a small relationship. In other words, date before marriage. And have a "prenuptial agreement" that gives you a clean way out if things don't go as expected.

Invest in tactics that are worth it

There are an infinite number of free and almost-free tactics. I hope the discussion of 25 of them in this and the previous chapter has stimulated your thinking about tactics that your company could use profitably. The next chapter, on "worth-it" tactics, will also help you prepare for Meeting 6.

Teach outside professionals about your business. If you don't sell your ad agency or designer, they can't sell your customers.

CHAPTER 8

TACTICS: WORTH IT

Y ou've thought about free and almost-free tactics. Now it's time to consider tactics that just plain cost money. We call this category "worth it," which means that if appropriate and well executed, these tactics can generate profits far beyond their cost. They also have the potential to absorb large amounts of money and return little or nothing, so it is critical to do them right or not at all.

Advertising

For most small and mid-size businesses, advertising means primarily print advertising. Many of these comments, however, apply equally to advertising on radio, cable TV, and the Internet. Whether you prepare and place your own ads or use an agency, it pays to develop your understanding of how to maximize the return on your advertising investment. There's an excellent book on the subject by advertising veteran Fred Hahn entitled *Do-It-Yourself Advertising: How to Produce Great Ads, Brochures, Catalogs, Direct Mail and Much More.* It's a Wiley Small Business Edition, available in paperback.

Are you planning to try one insertion of an ad, and continue if you get a response? Hahn and virtually every other authority on advertising agree that you'd be wasting your money. One insertion is not an adequate test of a display ad, particularly a business-to-business ad that does not involve running to the supermarket with a coupon. The minimum meaningful test is probably three insertions. Some say it takes six insertions in a monthly publication before people start to notice you. Repetition is the soul of advertising. Coke advertises on TV and in newspapers every day. Is there anybody who hasn't heard of Coke? Nevertheless, Coke reinforces its message by spending hundreds of millions of dollars on ads every year. Repetition is the soul of advertising.

The effect of advertising is cumulative. When we launched Abbey Rents Furniture, we did a lot of television advertising. Once we were established we reduced the frequency. Nevertheless, customers would walk in after we hadn't been on for several weeks and say, "I saw your ad on TV yesterday." The same will happen to you if you invest in good print ads and "buy and hold." After you run a 6x schedule for three years, people will tell you that they see your ad every month. The effect of advertising is cumulative.

Placing your ads in a prestige position—the back cover or an inside cover—at a reasonable additional cost can be well worth it. Readers see your ad more often and pay more attention to it because of its prominent location, so it increases the cumulative effect.

If you sell to other businesses, there are trade publications that reach your market. Their space rates are far less than those of consumer publications of equal stature. Take care to select exactly the right trade publication, as the best ad won't work if it reaches the wrong audience. Exactly who is your market? If you answer, "electronics manufacturers," is it computers, marine radar, aerospace instrumentation, or health-related devices? And do you sell to engineers, CFOs, or IT managers? Or maybe your market is HR people who read HR publications, not electronics journals. The best way to find out is to ask your present and potential customers what they read. Remember those "almost free" surveys we talked about? This could be a good question to include—but only if you are seriously considering trade advertising and/or placing articles in trade publications.

Trade advertising should be direct and clear. Do not allow your creative people, whether agency or in-house, to be so carried away with their ingenuity that the message is obscured. Your customers can turn the page in a second. A glance should tell them what you are selling and the chief benefit they will get from it. Then they can think, "I may need that, so I'll read the rest of this ad before I turn the page."

One client put an ad for a hot new product in *Builder's Journal.* Two days after the publication arrived he was disappointed because they hadn't received any responses. His reaction was not unusual. But ask yourself how many magazines and newsletters you received yesterday. Two? Three? Did you stop everything to read them, or are they in your "to read" pile? Are your customers any different? If your plan involves advertising, it should define the period of time over which you will evaluate the results. Otherwise, you may find yourself at the mercy of your emotions, like an investor who sells on a market downturn and then wishes he hadn't.

To put it another way, don't buy an ad. Plan a campaign.

Do you work with an ad agency? If so, it will help you get better and more cost-effective results to understand how agencies make their money. In most cases, it's from commissions on the purchase of print space or radio and TV time. The commission is generally stated as "15%," which it is, from the media point of view. If an agency buys $10,000 of space or time, their normal commission is $1,500. But from the advertiser's point of view, the commission is 17.65%. Why? Suppose you do your own advertising, and you request and get (you generally will) the 15% agency discount. You pay $8,500 for the "$10,000" space. If you go to an agency, you will have to pay an additional 17.65% of the $8,500 to reach $10,000. That's money you could put into copy writing and design.

Most agencies are not excited about trade advertising. Trade space rates are not low to you, because you are paying. But to an agency used to consumer space rates, trade rates are low, and the agency commission is therefore low. We've talked about how important it is to be proactive with all your vendors and to sell them on your company. This is perhaps more important with your ad agency than anyone else. Even if you are now a small client, the people working on your account must grasp your potential—must understand your story and your strategy—or they won't have the vision or motivation to produce effective ads.

Experienced, talented people frequently leave large agencies to start their own. If your company is small, consider hiring such an agency. You'll be an important client to them, and if you work well with them, you can grow together.

Don't start your relationship with an agency by saying, "We need advertising." Be prepared to tell an agency you are considering what your objectives are, and what publications you think you want to be in.

Your team should "get it" more and more as they work with you. They should come to you with ideas that make you say, "Why didn't I think of that?" If instead you find yourself repeatedly saying, "Wait a minute, I don't think that ad gets our message to our audience," it may be time to demand that different creative talent be assigned to your account, or even to look for another agency. But first, ask yourself if you've been managing the relationship well. Have you really invested in teaching the agency about your business and in developing relationships with them? If not, you're going to put time, effort, and money into switching agencies, and the results are unlikely to be an improvement.

How much should you spend to create a trade ad? Over the years, I've developed a formula: production should not exceed 10% of space. Uh, oh. An ad, especially if it involves models and a quality photo shoot (and there is no point in showing your market mediocre pictures of your product) can easily cost $10,000 to produce. If the space costs $3,000 per insertion, and it's a monthly publication, you'd have to run the ad for 33 months to comply with the formula. I doubt that you will want to run the same ad for almost three years!

Repetition may be the soul of advertising, but boredom is its death. So how can you justify the production cost? Here are some ways:

- Use the same ad in other publications.

- Use the ad, or variations on it, for other purposes: direct mail, sell sheets, handouts when you give a talk, literature tables.

- Use HTML versions of the ad, or elements of the ad, on your Web site or for advertising on other Web sites.

Desks in the desert sun

At Anderson Desk a 2-day photo shoot for an ad campaign involved driving a truckload of office furniture to the desert. The lighting was magnificent. The photographer was an inspired pro, with a day rate to match. How did we justify this expensive shoot? Our plan called for using one of the photographs on 23 different ads and collateral marketing pieces. And we did.

Consumer advertising is expensive. It can be profitable, or a waste of money. You cannot measure its value unless you know what your return is. At Abbey Rents Furniture, we knew that if we advertised on TV with 200 gross rating points one week, 100 the next, and 100 the next, our walk-ins doubled. How did we know this rather precise piece of information? We kept track of walk-in traffic every day in every store. Store staff didn't like this tedious chore. "Why do I have to do that, John?" "Because I need the information. And because you need your job." We went through the same process with a client in the paging business. They would change their ads, their frequency, their locations, without a clue as to what worked and what didn't. So we established a policy: "We have to know what our advertising is producing. Anybody who doesn't make a hash mark when we get a walk-in customer has made a career decision, even if you are the best salesperson in the world."

When you know how many walk-ins there are, and you know the number and size of your sales, you can calculate your closing ratio in transactions and dollars. Those numbers reveal the value of your advertising, and allow you to determine if a change in advertising is positive or negative. Of course you have to be careful to change only one thing at a time and to adjust for seasons and whatever other factors extraneous to the ads may affect your business.

When you are selling to businesses, the equivalent to tracking walk-ins is tracking bids and proposals. You have to track successful proposals and "lost business" as the first step in figuring out what worked and what didn't. You know you have improved your marketing and sales process when your closing ratio goes up.

How fast does advertising have to pay for itself? It depends. Once you've achieved a level of recognition, retail advertising should pay for itself on a 1-to-1 basis. In other words, if you are running an ad every day or every week, it should pay for itself, on the average, every day or every week. What if you are selling big-ticket items to businesses and the typical sales cycle is 18 months? Here, the advertising is more of a long-term investment. Still, after enough time has elapsed you can evaluate it based on your numbers.

Look for ways to leverage your advertising dollars. Can you partner with a strategic ally who is better known than you and has access to a group of customers you want? Would you be better off investing in your partner's advertising than doing your own? There are myriad possibilities. Based on consulting with over 400 companies, I've found that the two most common mistakes are to advertise too little rather than too much, and to try to get by with mediocre ads rather than investing in excellent ads.

Direct mail

In direct mail, whether to individual consumers or businesses, you are out to make the sale based on the material in the direct-mail package (or packages if you are sending a series). It's a science, based on measurement. A reasonable return pays for itself. If you are not basing your direct-mail campaign on carefully thought out numerical projections, you are well on your way to wasting a lot of money. Write out a check and mail it directly to yourself instead. When you get a 3% return rate, which would normally justify a victory celebration, it is not the time to discover that you needed a 10% rate (which is virtually impossible) for the campaign to break even.

Direct mail is one area where you should almost undoubtedly outsource. Work with professionals who understand tapes, lists, sorts, postal regulations, fulfillment, and especially how to get people to read your package rather than deposit it in the trash. They will also know how to test a mailing by using a small percentage of a list, and how to try out different price points. Take the time to learn about these things, but find a partner who has already mastered the details.

If the campaign works, you're going to keep using direct mail. Sell the direct-mail house on your company, your people, your products and services. Clearly state your objectives, including the rate of return you have to achieve. A professional, experienced direct-mail house won't let you sign up for a campaign with unreachable goals. The friction costs of working with a 1-time client are too great. Direct-mail houses make money by developing clients who come back again and again, and learn the routine. For them to profit, you have to profit.

When planning a direct-mail campaign, consider soft goals as well as hard goals. The hard goal is the return rate, the number of orders. Soft goals can include spreading out the costs by giving the same materials, or variations on them, to your salespeople, your employees, your present customers, your strategic allies. You might also provide alternative methods of purchase. For example, if you're selling a book, in addition to the 800 number and fax/mail order form, you might indicate that the book is available at local bookstores or on the Internet.

Telephone marketing

I don't call it telemarketing, because that word has been given a bad name by the script readers who call you up at dinner time and want you to switch your long distance service or extend your warranty. I'm talking about real marketing with the telephone. Little Earth Productions created displays for the fashion accessories it makes from recycled materials. Then the question was how to get stores, especially stores in resort area shops, to take the displays. The goal was to add $1 million in sales by putting 1,000 displays into stores, with the average display producing $1,000 a year for Little Earth. The tactic was to hire a professional telephone marketing firm and pay them well—but only for results. So Little Earth risked no cash.

The biggest problem in using the telephone to market is reaching people. It seems as though you reach voicemail five time as often as a live person. What should you do if you are following up with someone you've already spoken to or sent material to, someone who has previously expressed interest, but they never call you back? First of all, don't take it personally. Overcome "seller's paranoia." The person you're trying to reach may be overwhelmed by a project with a tight deadline, an illness in the family, or any one of a number of things that take their attention away from you and your products or services. Sure, it's in their interest to buy now. But their agenda is not your agenda.

Second, don't give up if you believe your product or service makes sense for the potential customer. If the reason they are not getting back to you may have nothing to do with you, it makes sense to keep trying. Research has shown that most salespeople quit before getting to yes, without ever getting a "no."

Third, be creative. Leave explicit, interesting voice mail messages. Send faxes or email. Look for gimmicks. I'm a wine lover. If I know your thing is wine, I might send you a bottle. Or maybe a wine label, with a suggestion to try this. Or I might send you an invitation to a seminar I'm giving, or an article I think will be useful to you.

Their agenda is not your agenda

Hunter Douglas is an international manufacturer and marketer of window fashions—blinds, shades, draperies. They had expressed interest in hiring me to consult and conduct clinics in many of their locations. To follow up this major opportunity I called and called, and even visited their headquarters in Upper Saddle River, New Jersey. That's a round trip from LA to New York, a car rental, and a hotel stay—all at my expense—for a one-hour visit. I did that three times! For six months they never called back. Finally I crossed them off my follow-up list. "John, you're crazy!" I said to myself when I thought of those three trips. Then Hunter Douglas called. I had the urge to respond, "Why now? I've written you off!" But I'm not that wealthy. It turned into ongoing major business.

Sometimes, especially if it's not the biggest piece of business in the world, I let it all out. I'll leave a message like, "I wrote the proposal for you in 24 hours, as you requested. The terms work for the budget you outlined. I've left three messages for you over a period of three weeks. Is it too much to ask for you to call back? Even just to explain why you've decided not to use my services." Once in a while this approach helps land a job. And it's always satisfying.

Regular communications

"Out of sight, out of mind." A newsletter or some other form of regular communication with customers, potential customers, allies, and referral sources keeps you in mind. To enhance your image, your newsletter should be

- Unique to your business (not canned copy with your name stuck on)

- Informative and educational (not straight sales copy)

- Attractive and well written

225

- On schedule

- At least quarterly (to maintain repetition value)

How many times have you heard business people say, "We've tried to have a newsletter, but we never manage to get it out regularly." Why not? If we're writing the plan in October, and we say a newsletter has to go out February 8, May 8, August 8, and November 8, why shouldn't it happen? Do we follow the plan, or do we run around putting out fires and lose out on a valuable sales tool that increases in value as it continues?

A newsletter does not have to be done in-house. Just write one word, "newsletter," on a file folder. When something exciting comes across your desk, put a copy in the folder. If you land an important new customer, or do something special with an existing customer, make a note and throw it in the folder. A customer writes a letter about what great job so and so in customer service did; the letter goes in the folder. Your outside writer picks up the material, interviews you and whomever else needs to be interviewed (employees, clients, associates), and submits the draft for your review. Rick's firm does newsletters. As they learn what your company is all about, they become proactive, suggesting topics that would make good articles for your readers. And they force you to stay on schedule.

Take your writer to lunch, get newsletter for dessert
Haskell of Pittsburgh put out a newsletter for 30 years. Even though we were a $30 million company with 500 employees, my father found it cost effective to outsource the newsletter. About 10 years into it, through Service Corps of Retired Executives (SCORE), he found Norton Webber, a former senior advertising executive. Norton came over once a quarter, picked up Dad's newsletter folder, and Dad would take him out to lunch and they'd talk. A week later, Dad got the newsletter. All laid out. After a while, Norton worked directly with our ad agency on the layout. Dad's total invested time in the newsletter was lunch. Norton became the voice of

the company. He was a good listener, and he could get the Haskell message and style down on paper better than anybody.

Your newsletter does not have to be an elaborate, expensive production. Content is king. I sent my article, "The 5 Worst Mistakes in Marketing and Sales," to 4,800 people. One sheet, two sides, two colors. I got more response from it than anything else I've ever sent out. Am I going to write and circulate similar pieces? What do you think?

It doesn't always have to be your own material. If you see a great article, and you send it to customers, potential customers, and referral sources with a note about why you think it will help them, they will appreciate it. Just make sure to get permission from whomever holds the copyright. In many cases, they will be happy to give you permission in return for the publicity they'll get on your postage stamp.

If emailing your newsletter works for your market, that can reduce the distribution cost to zero. Get permission from each recipient, so that they don't feel you are "spamming" them, and give them an easy way to get off the list. Pay as much attention to the content and style as if you were printing the newsletter and mailing it out.

Use the material in your newsletter to refresh your Web site, and offer it to related but non-competing Web sites in return for links to your site.

Long-term graphics source

We've already talked about working with an ad agency. Depending on the size and nature of your business, you may not need an ad agency or have the budget for one. No matter what the size or nature of your business, though, you almost certainly need graphic design for your logo, letterheads and business cards; for flyers, brochures, and ads; for packaging.

If your marketing department puts out a steady stream of material in-house, it's worth it to have software programs such as Quark,

PageMaker, Freehand, and PhotoShop. Your people will be using them enough to get reasonably proficient and efficient. Otherwise, don't waste your money buying and updating these programs. People design, not programs.

The highest and best use of your time is not doing a flyer or brochure. Even if your marketing people do quick, routine stuff, for major pieces you are better off with a professional designer.

Designers like to create beauty. Be sure the beauty delivers your message to your customers. If you're pitching eye glasses to senior citizens, don't use 6-point type and images that appeal to 25-year-olds, which may well be the age of the designer. (Don't use tiny type for anybody! Designers often set type in small sizes because it "gets in the way" of the overall image. The only problem is nobody reads your copy.)

Whoever in your company works with the design firm will be more effective if they know something about design. A good source is a paperback book by Robin Williams called *The Non-Designer's Design Book*. Ms. Williams explains four simple design principles visually and in crystal clear English. Understand the design firm as well. Whether it's a 1-person outfit or a large company, they're in business to make a profit. Do not expect them to spend hours or days on your brochure for peanuts. You don't always get what you pay for, but you almost never get what you don't pay for.

Everything we've said about relating to advertising agencies and other outside professionals applies equally to designers. Be proactive, sell them on your company, get them excited about your potential. You're trying to develop a partner as well as to get a particular job done. You don't want to start every new job from scratch. A design firm that is excited about your business may create a wonderful graphic that you will use for 10 years. They never get paid for that, just for the job in which it happened. That's the nature of the graphics business. It happens with advertising copy too. I came up with the phrase "Run Tiger!" for Asics Tiger shoes. I didn't know that it translates into every language in the world. Mr. Unisaka, Asics' president, came from Japan to the US for a sales meeting, held up our poster of a man and woman and a live tiger running at sunset on the beach at Malibu, and yelled "Run Tiger!" That's the only English he ever spoke in his life! But he could express the same thing in France and everywhere else that he went. We thought we were going to go through 10,000 posters. We did—in the first month. I wish I had a few cents for every "Run Tiger!" poster Asics printed.

Why did that phrase pop into my mind? And why did my associates at Professional Marketing Group realize that phrase was the right one? Because as a result of working with Asics day in and day out for months on other projects, we became their partner, we understood their business. In a sense, they got the phrase for nothing. Looking at it from their viewpoint, that's part of what they paid us for all those months. They tripled sales the year of the "Run Tiger!" campaign.

Market Research

You've seen the power of even a crude, anecdotally developed competitive matrix. Imagine how much more powerful a competitive matrix could be if it were based on sound, quantified information about how your products and your competitors' products are positioned in the market, and why consumers decide to buy theirs or yours.

Getting that kind of information means hiring experienced, professional market researchers. This is expensive, but it may be more than worth it. How many of you use Quicken? One reason Quicken emerged as the market leader is that they did a tremendous amount of research on what consumers wanted in personal finance software, and on how to market to them. Intuit, the company behind Quicken software, even has a special area of their Web site devoted to getting product improvement suggestions from their user base. They also solicit stories on how customers use their products.

There's qualitative and quantitative research. Focus groups are one way of conducting qualitative research. A professional interviewer talks to a group of potential users of a product or service. Observers watch through a one-way mirror or via video. Copywriters love focus groups, because many times the participants will write their headlines for them. Whiting's is a famous dairy in the Chicago area. At a school board meeting, a number of dairies were pitching to be selected as the milk vendor for the school system. One parent stood up and said, "This decision is a no-brainer. 'Whiting's' on milk is like sterling on silver." A Whiting's employee wrote that down, and it became the company's tagline. That was at a public meeting, but it happens all the time in focus groups. Somebody will say something that sparks a campaign for the next 10 years.

Can you save money by running your own focus groups instead of hiring market research professionals? In a word, no. When someone with a vested interest is involved, you get a brainstorming session, at best. At worst, you get the answers you want, which you already had without spending a penny. I was watching a focus group through a one-way mirror with my client. The client didn't like the way the moderator was leading it, so he ran into the room and took over. He browbeat the participants into agreeing that his company's product was the best.

Within this absurd misuse of a focus group lies a nugget of truth. Just as with surveys, there is no use having focus groups unless you intend to use the results to make decisions. We had decided to improve our product based on the outcome of this and other focus groups. Unfortunately, my client decided to "improve" the outcome of the focus group instead.

Focus groups are limited by their qualitative nature, and by the fact that they can be skewed by one or two strong personalities (although a good moderator will encourage everybody to express their views and prevent anyone from dominating the group).

Quantitative research involves surveys of one kind or another, to discover the demographics of buyers and potential buyers, and/or what they are thinking (their individual responses, uninfluenced by the flow of a group discussion). The surveys may be conducted in person, online, or by phone, fax, or mail.

As we discussed earlier, you can do simple surveys on your own, although it helps to have a professional review your questions and evaluate the statistical results. At a certain point, it pays to call in the market research pros for surveys. Again, when designing the survey, make sure that the answers will lead to decisions, even if it's a decision not to develop a product or service, or not to use a particular method of promotion.

Public relations
In Chapter 6 we talked about do-it-yourself PR.

If you can afford it, however, hiring a good PR firm can do wonders to promote your company and its people, products and services.

PR firms have also been known to grow fat on monthly retainers while contributing little in the way of tangible results.

Once you've selected the right firm, proactive management is the key. Everything we wrote about working with advertising agencies and design firms applies equally to PR firms. You must sell your PR firm on your company, or they cannot possibly sell your company to your public.

Go in with quantifiable objectives in mind. Do you want to host a social event four times a year that attracts key customers, potential customers, centers of influence, and the media? Tell them. Do you want your products reviewed in each of three trade journals that serve your three markets? Tell them. Do you want to appear on Oprah? Tell them. They may respond that your goals are unrealistic, inappropriate, or even too low, but at least give them a place to start.

Before signing a contract with any PR firm, insist on meeting the people who will actually work on your behalf, and if you are not satisfied, then or later, say so. Sometimes you'll hire a firm because you are impressed with its track record and with its principals, only to find that interns or recent college graduates are assigned to your account. This is not necessarily bad; if their youthful energy and creativity is properly supervised by experienced pros, the results may be excellent. But they may not be, and in any case it should not come as an unpleasant surprise that your frontline PR troops are just out of basic training. Of course, if your market is young people, it's vital to have people on your PR and advertising teams who are part of that market.

Refine tactics

As outlined in the Meeting Agendas, in Meeting 6 you imagine a wide variety of free, almost-free, and worth-it tactics that could help you achieve your marketing and sales goals.

After Meeting 6, each team member selects two tactics that he or she believes are the best of the bunch, and comes to Meeting 7 prepared to make a case for them. Your case should include details of how the tactics would be carried out, who will carry them out, and why they are feasible and cost effective. (Remember Sally and the veggiedog mobile at the beginning of Chapter 6?)

Complete your plan

Once you've selected your tactics for the coming year, your plan requires only a marketing and sales budget and calendar to be complete. The next chapter is your guide to creating those vital tools.

Your calendar and budget integrate your tactics into a coherent whole. They help you make adjustments for feasibility, affordability, and return on investment.

CHAPTER 9

MAKE A CALENDAR AND BUDGET

On time. Complete. Within budget. These are words you want to be able to use at your quarterly evaluations or when you look back at your marketing and sales plan a year from now. That way, you will be able to determine how well your tactics worked—not how well they might have worked if they had been carried out properly.

"On time" means that tactics are carried out on the schedule you set up to maximize their effectiveness. Within the limits of the possible "on time" also means without crash projects, which cause costly errors and extra expenses such as overtime.

"Complete" means that all aspects of the tactic are done right the first time. For example, when the Canter Video Library was launched, the packaged 3-tape set, the individually packaged tapes, the brochure, fliers, price list, and mailing lists were simultaneously ready on schedule. Today this would include all the elements of online promotion as well.

"Within budget" means that tactic A was carried out without killing the funds meant for tactics B and C. It also means that if tactic A achieves the expected (or better) results, you will realize the expected (or better) return on investment.

235

How do you write your plan to achieve "on time," "complete," and "within budget"?

Calendar + Budget = Recipe for success

Read the recipe for your favorite dish. It lists the ingredients and outlines the method for cooking them before reaching those magic words, "Serves 4."

By setting goals, you've identified the dishes you want to create. By selecting tactics, you've assembled the ingredients.

Now you're ready to combine the tactics so that you can carry them out step by step, at the right time and in the right order, to serve up a great result. These final elements in your plan are the equivalent of the cooking instructions in your recipe. They are the

- Marketing and sales calendar

- Marketing and sales budget

The calendar and budget integrate your tactics into a coherent whole that is greater than the sum of its parts. They also provide additional perspectives—time and money—from which to evaluate your decisions and make final adjustments for feasibility, affordability, and potential return on investment.

Reality check

Your marketing and sales calendar is critical to getting real buy-in from your staff and from partners such as strategic allies, suppliers, customers, ad agencies, PR firms, design firms, writers, Web designers, and direct-mail houses. The calendar goes beyond general agreement to responsibility for delivering particular projects (and stages of projects) on particular dates. By summarizing all your marketing and sales activities in one place, the calendar reveals conflicts (you'll all be at a trade show the same week you are supposed to select the direction for the new ad campaign) and contradictions (one of your tactics is to build relationships in a trade association, but no one is assigned to go the monthly meetings, participate in a committee, or have lunch with the members).

Your marketing and sales budget is critical to getting buy-in from top management and from outside sources of finance. Even if you are top management and your funds are internally generated, your budget helps prevent you from committing unrealistic—or inadequate—sums to marketing and sales. By summarizing all your marketing and sales expenses in one place, the budget quickly reveals imbalances (a new product with high potential is receiving insufficient support, while a cash cow that will soon be obsolete has an inflated advertising budget left over from earlier years).

You save time by working on the calendar and budget together because they are different slices of the same data. Each tactic goes on the calendar, and most tactics have at least a small expense associated with them.

You gain insight by considering the budget and calendar together. For example, your calendar shows that you are going to be advertising in a trade publication every month next year and that you are participating in a national conference sponsored by that publication. The budget shows you are paying full price for the conference and that while you are getting the 12-insertion price for your full-page color ads, you have forgotten to request the 15% agency discount (you do your own advertising, with the help of a design firm). You decide to request the discount and good ad placement, negotiate about the conference fee, and perhaps ask for a free banner on the publication's Web site. You may also request the publication to lock in your advertising rate for the following year, an easy concession for them to make now that could be valuable to you 14 months later. You also make a note to talk to your PR firm (or your internal PR person) about how easy it would be to get editorial coverage in this publication, and the best way to utilize such coverage.

The marketing and sales calendar is the ultimate feasibility check and guide. We're going to a trade show six months from now. We've identified the relevant opportunities and tactics. What must happen this week, next week, and next month so we'll be ready to implement our tactics? And who is responsible for meeting these deadlines? All that information goes on the calendar, where those who lead marketing and sales can check on it, day by day, week by week, month by month.

The calendar can be surprisingly revealing. When Health for Life worked on its calendar, it discovered it had to change the way it operated. The publisher of health and fitness books had the opportunity to expand its offerings. In the past, they had edited their books internally. When they put publication dates on their calendar and worked backwards, it was apparent that they could not follow their existing model and get the books out on schedule. Accordingly, they hired outside editing resources, which their budget showed would provide good return on investment.

For a small paging company, the budget was the revelation. Their severe problem was turnover in the sales force, which they wanted to correct by increasing their salespeople's compensation. The budget showed that even with the expected increase in sales from more stable and more motivated salespeople, the extra compensation simply wasn't there. "Aha," they said, "Let's add a line of accessories that our salespeople can sell, with each accessory carrying a spiff, so that the extra compensation flows from additional revenue."

Marketing and sales calendar

The next three pages show what a 2-month slice of your marketing and sales calendar might look like. For simplicity, we've followed just one activity: getting out the May 1999 issue of the quarterly newsletter. This is an established newsletter, so there is no need to include searching for suitable outside resources and getting bids.

veggiedog Marketing & Sales Calendar
Newsletter Entries

April

Thursday	1	
Friday	2	
Saturday	3	
Sunday	4	
Monday	5	
Tuesday	6	
Wednesday	7	**EVERYONE** Deadline for submitting newsletter article ideas to Ginger
Thursday	8	
Friday	9	*Newsletter* Ginger meets with Stan & Madelyn to decide newsletter content; alerts those to be interviewed
Saturday	10	
Sunday	11	
Monday	12	
Tuesday	13	
Wednesday	14	*Newsletter* Ginger gives info to Rob; Rob sets up interviews, starts writing
Thursday	15	
Friday	16	
Saturday	17	
Sunday	18	
Monday	19	
Tuesday	20	
Wednesday	21	
Thursday	22	
Friday	23	
Saturday	24	
Sunday	25	
Monday	26	
Tuesday	27	
Wednesday	28	
Thursday	29	
Friday	30	

veggiedog Marketing & Sales Calendar
Newsletter Entries

May

Saturday	1	
Sunday	2	
Monday	3	**Newsletter** Ginger receives first draft from Rob
Tuesday	4	**Newsletter** Ginger gets back to Rob with suggested changes
Wednesday	5	
Thursday	6	**Newsletter** Ginger receives second draft from Rob
Friday	7	**Newsletter** Ginger makes any required final tweaks
Saturday	8	
Sunday	9	
Monday	10	**Newsletter** Ginger sends final copy to Linda
Tuesday	11	
Wednesday	12	
Thursday	13	**Newsletter** Ginger and Rob receive layout from Linda, Ginger suggests changes after conferring with Rob
Friday	14	**Newsletter** Ginger receives corrected layout
Saturday	15	
Sunday	16	
Monday	17	**Newsletter** Ginger signs off on final layout
Tuesday	18	**EVERYONE** Deadline for submitting new names or corrections for mailing list to Harvey
Wednesday	19	**Newsletter** Camera ready copy received by printer (Ginger confirms) Linda sends electronic file to Harvey (Ginger confirms)

veggiedog Marketing & Sales Calendar
Newsletter Entries

Continued

Thursday	*20*	*Newsletter*
		Printer makes plates (Ginger confirms)
Friday	*21*	*Newsletter*
		Printed (Ginger does press check)
Saturday	*22*	
Sunday	*23*	
Monday	*24*	
Tuesday	*25*	*Newsletter*
		Folded (Ginger confirms)
		Labels printed (Harvey)
		Temp agency called (Harvey)
Wednesday	*26*	*Newsletter*
		Folded newsletters picked up
		at printer (Ginger)
Thursday	*27*	*Newsletter*
		Labels, postage affixed (Harvey, temps)
		Newsletter to Post Office (Harvey)
Friday	*28*	*Newsletter*
		Content posted on Web site (Harvey)
Saturday	*29*	
Sunday	*30*	
Monday	*31*	

Ginger, assistant marketing director, is responsible for the newsletter. She prepared these calendar entries by working backward from May 28, the day the newsletter is supposed to go to the post office. Knowing that things can go wrong, Ginger built cushions throughout the plan, including scheduling May 27 as the concluding day.

Obviously, Ginger has to have all these dates on her personal calendar. And Rob, the outside writer; Linda, the outside designer; Harvey, who is in charge of data base (and therefore of the newsletter mailing list); and the outside printer each have to know their dates. But does the overall marketing and sales calendar require so much detail?

You'll have to work out the best solution for your company, which will probably involve some trial and error. On the one hand, you don't want to overwhelm everyone in marketing, sales, and customer service. For example, they don't need to know the individual steps of the printing process. On the other hand, you want to make everybody in the company conscious of the newsletter as a sales and marketing tool. Therefore the entries headed "EVERYONE" about deadlines for submitting story ideas and names for the mailing list should certainly be on the overall calendar. And Madelyn, the head of marketing, should have access to all the steps, so she can check up on Ginger, and make sure that the process goes forward if for any reason Ginger is unavailable.

Publish or perish (share the calendar)

Let's leave the newsletter for a moment and take up the general question of sharing the calendar. How many times in October and November do employees ask, "Are we off the Friday after Thanksgiving?" Since you know the answer, or could easily know it, a year ahead of time, why not make it easy for your employees to plan their lives by publishing it then?

Now let's extend the logic. Why not share with your employees next year's important marketing and sales events, the events that you want them to plan their business lives around? If you employees, particularly your best, most self-directed employees, have this information, isn't it likely that they will act to enhance the tactics you've selected? Even if you elect not to share other parts of the plan, I strongly advocate wide dissemination of the marketing and sales calendar.

Back to the newsletter. Why is so much air built into the early part of the schedule? First of all, why not? It's a quarterly newsletter, so why not take advantage of the available time? Secondly, the newsletter features articles based on interviews with customers: executives of supermarket chains, supermarket managers, and even individual consumers. Once Ginger meets with Madelyn and Stan, the CEO, to decide on the stories, she has to contact the interviewees to get their consent. Then Rob, the writer, has to have time to set up the telephone interviews. Ginger has built in time so that even if the interviewees are out of town on business or vacation, the newsletter will still be published on schedule. If things go smoothly and it's ready early, so much the better.

Calendar code

How can Ginger, Harvey, and others separate the newsletter entries from other data on the full marketing and sales calendar?

This calendar was prepared using the calendar template feature of Microsoft Word. Conveniently, each day is a cell which elongates as you insert more data. Here are some ways to make calendar information easy to use with Word or other programs, including dedicated project management programs. Many of the same ideas apply to large master calendars prepared by hand.

- Always use a heading that identifies the project. In this case, the heading is "Newsletter" except for the two "EVERYONE" headings, designed to get the attention of employees who might disregard "Newsletter" because it is not their responsibility. In those two cases, "newsletter" is in the entry. So anybody can track the steps of the newsletter project simply by searching for "newsletter."

243

- Use a distinctive color and/or typestyle for each project or type of project

- Use the search feature to find assignments you are responsible for by searching for your name.

Of course, with project management software, if you have set things up right, you can view and print out the entries for each project separately from the entries for all other projects.

A calendar you could count on

A sales meeting 10 weeks before the start of each quarter was a crucial element of the Lykes Meat Group turnaround plan. At these meetings, every salesperson received a complete package which included materials for
- marketing
- merchandising
- advertising
- promotion
- sales
- public relations
- self-directed sales management

The Lykes program succeeded because the commitment to having everything ready for this meeting was kept quarter after quarter for two years. During the first few quarters there was a "wait-and-see" attitude in the minds of salespeople and customers. By the third quarter we saw that the salespeople and through them, the customers, were beginning to count on our programs and to build around them. By the end of the 4th quarter we had turned the company from an $18 million annual loss to break even. Continuing with the programs led to profitability. The innovation and creativity that went into the programs was essential to building excitement around them, but without the calendar and the consistency it generated, the programs would have been just another paper campaign that fails to doesn't produce real-world results.

Which calendar is right for you?

The calendar is the calendar, right? Not necessarily. The calendar can be any number of different calendars.

Fiscal year vs. calendar year

At Westhoff Machinery in St. Louis the calendar was a major issue. The company had defined its fiscal year as October 1 through September 30. This arrangement had been created years before by the accountants. And their software was set up to report only in that way.

Unfortunately, management had never considered the impact of the fiscal year on marketing and sales. It turned out that reports running from October 1 made it difficult to analyze sales. Many salespeople couldn't relate to the results, let alone forecast for upcoming quarters. They planned their lives based on January through December. Everybody understands the calendar year. Any other basis requires extra thinking. When Westhoff changed its fiscal year to conform to the calendar year, it was much easier to involve its people in the planning and forecasting process.

Accounting firms often put small companies on a fiscal year that does not start January 1 because it is more convenient for the CPAs. Unfortunately, many small company owners go along with this because they figure their accountants know best. I feel safe advising smaller company management to run their business on a calendar fiscal year. It pays off. The CPAs may not like making the change, but unless they can provide a compelling reason not to, it's worth it.

5-4-4 Calendar

In larger companies the accounting department often creates a quarterly calendar based on assigning whole weeks to each month such that each quarter has the correct number (13) weeks. Each quarter has one 5-week month and two 4-week months, always in the same order to facilitate meaningful comparison to the same month in a different year. The most typical order is 5-4-4, although 4-4-5 is also used. One advantage of this type of calendar is that the month always ends on a Friday. Mid-week cutoffs often create problems for internal accounting departments. Ending the month on a Friday provides time to get the closing figures done quickly.

5-4-4 makes it easy to compare data. Every month has either 25 business days or 20 business days. This feature can also simplify planning.

Plan to plan

Your marketing and sales plan should include a series of entries for completing the next annual marketing and sales plan. By blocking in your eight meetings now, along with anything else that's required, you demonstrate your ongoing commitment to the planning process. By putting planning first on the agenda, a year ahead of time, you make planning easier. Everybody builds the rest of their schedule around the commitment to plan. Planning, the most important activity, is no longer an afterthought to be fit in around everything else.

Assuming that you are working on a calendar year, your calendar should be completed and ready to publish no later than October 31. Regardless of whether you are that far ahead on your first marketing and sales plan, your plan for next year should include that deadline. That means you should start the 8-week planning process in late August or the first week of September. If data will be required that could hold up the process, schedule assignments to assemble that data accordingly.

Completion of the next year's marketing and sales plan must precede completion of that year's overall business plan and overall budget. Without top line (sales) data, there can be no meaningful business plan. With the exception of funds raised by financing, budgets are 100% dependent on sales levels. Why? Because sales produce gross profit. Gross profit is often defined as "contribution margin," which refers to the amount of money available to cover the costs of selling and general and administrative expenses (SGA).

Live with your plan

How often do you look at something you wrote a week ago or a month ago and say, "Here's how it could have been better"?

By finishing your plan between October 31 and mid-November, you have six to eight weeks to review it, live with it, digest it, and think about it. That allows you to make adjustments based on cash flow, special events, unique circumstances, or any of the thousands of other things that may happen. Or just waking up one morning and having what seems like a refinement or better idea.

A word of caution. At the very least, get input from the other members of the planning team on your "better idea." It may not be better than what the team worked out, because of factors you've overlooked. And even if it is better, unilateral adoption will, in the long run, undermine the planning process.

Long term plans

Wouldn't it be wonderful to have a 3- or 5-year plan? The reality of smaller businesses is that getting even a 1-year plan done can seem like a miracle. Ninety-five percent of companies do not have a written plan. Joining the 5% that do is your profit prescription. The results will speak for themselves. As your company develops, you may see your way to writing a 24-month plan. That would be great, even though it will undoubtedly require modification as the second year draws closer.

Most smaller companies cannot create a meaningful comprehensive marketing and sales plan beyond a 2-year horizon. Too many changes will take place over 24 months. At a certain point, what has the appearance of planning becomes speculation. It looks like Mom's apple pie, but it's really pie in the sky.

Marketing and sales budget

Even the sound of the word "budget" suggests hard-nosed, no-nonsense facts. Marketing people use budgets to show top management and accounting that they too inhabit the precise world of numbers and spreadsheets.

Ha! I have seen more fantasy and wish fulfillment in marketing and sales budgets than in advertising campaigns. Many marketing people would get far better results if they applied the imagination they put into budgets to promotion, and the cut-and-dry approach they take to marketing to budgets.

How to make real estimates

Why are budgets so frequently—and so far—off the mark? My clients tell me of projects where their cost overruns have been over 100%. Think about missing by 100%. That's as if you set out to fly from New York to Los Angeles and landed in Honolulu.

The single biggest reason for such discrepancies is the attempt to estimate the costs of projects when the projects themselves are not yet clearly defined. "We want a brochure." Well, what size? How many pages? How many colors? How many photos and/or illustrations? How much new writing? How much research? What's the print run? On what kind of stock? Will there be more than one version? How will it be distributed? How long will it be used? Will there be inserts, a cover letter, several different cover letters? Will there be service bureau charges, sales tax, and shipping fees? The list could go on, and a similar list could be made for an ad campaign, a Web site, a promotion, or any other tactic.

You might think that guestimates based on ill-defined projects would average out, because they'd have as much chance of being too low as too high. That's logical, but false. In real life, people want to be able to afford things, so they estimate low, and tend to forget "extras" such as taxes and shipping. Furthermore, they ask outside vendors for "ballpark figures which I won't hold you to." Many vendors will quote based on no-frills, low-end specs, to fulfill their own wishes of not pricing themselves out of the job. Even when smarter and more responsible vendors quote a range, the low numbers tend to end up in the ever-hopeful budget projections.

To get reality-based budget entries, think your projects through in detail. Include outside vendors in the thinking before you ask them for estimates.

Writing a marketing and sales plan, with a marketing and sales calendar, is a huge advantage here, because you build in adequate lead time to define the project.

Fear of spending

Guestimates tend to result in spending far more than expected.

Another kind of mistake results in failure to make profitable investments in marketing. It works like this. A company is considering putting up a Web site, or upgrading its present site. A good Web design firm says a site that will do what's needed will cost about $20K. The company executives say, "Wow. That's a lot of money. We have the $20K, but we sure don't want to spend that much on a Web site." They decide not to do the project at all, or perhaps to invest $4K in a scaled-down version.

We could call this mistake "thinking from the wrong end"—of the financials, that is. The company never considered how much additional revenue the Web site might help produce, over what period of time. Without evaluating the potential return, they arbitrarily decided $20K was too much to spend. They might justify spending the $4K by thinking, "It's only 20% of what we might have spent." But what if the $20K could reasonably have been expected to produce $80K in added value over the next two years, while the $4K could reasonably be expected to produce nothing, or even to be a competitive disadvantage? In that case, isn't it the $4K that is "too much to spend," not the $20K? It's great to find a genuine bargain on something that meets your needs, but a good saying to keep in mind is, "There's no right price for the wrong product."

Bean counters cannot run marketing

The poster of a beautiful young couple running on the beach at sunset with a live tiger helped boost US sales of Tiger Shoes 50% in one quarter. We had budgeted the "Run Tiger!" poster for 20,000 copies, which we thought, based on reports from the management and sales force, would last a year, when it would be time for another campaign.

The posters flew out of the store room. After a few trade shows, consumer exhibitions, and other activities we realized that the 20,000 posters would not last through the first quarter. We suggested a re-run. US Tiger management responded, "It's not in the budget." They did not want to report to corporate headquarters in Japan that they were going to spend $40K for an item budgeted at $20K. It did not matter to that the posters contributed to a 1-quarter increase in sales of over $500K and an increase in gross profits of over $150K, and that additional posters would likely add to that trend. Only the expense mattered. The knew the numbers, but did not grasp their relationship to value added.

How much should we spend on marketing?

In many industries there are accepted figures for the correct amount of revenue to spend on marketing. Three percent might be the figure for your industry. The idea is that if you spend less, you won't be getting the word out enough to maintain or expand your market share, and that if you spend more, it will cut too deeply into profits. Often there is a lot of validity to these figures, which are based on decades of positive and negative experience of many companies.

But, let the seller beware.

First, things change, with ever increasing rapidity. Are you even sure what industry you are in? Is that industry defined the same way it was ten years ago (assuming that it existed ten years ago)? Even more important, how will it be defined next year? And is the level of direct and indirect competition the same? Percentages considered correct based on past experience may no longer be valid under the new conditions. Would we have heard of Amazon.com if they had followed the rules on marketing expenses set by previous book retailers? Those marketers who best perceive the new trends and grasp their implications are the marketers that win.

Second, general truths about how much to spend on marketing may not apply to your particular company at a particular moment in its development. Say we are starting a boutique accounting, legal, or other professional services firm. Projected revenue for the coming year is $1 million, and our overall guideline for marketing expenditures is 3%, or $30,000.

We want to use the following tactics: brochures and other collateral literature (including development of an effective logo), a PR program (including participation in local events), joining a networking organization, and launching a Web site. We'll publicize our URL through all our activities, so a really good Web site will enhance the value of everything else we do, and vice versa.

We develop detailed plans for each tactic. The total comes to $60K, not $30K. Six percent of anticipated revenue, not three percent.

If the additional revenue will not be available, we have to change our plan accordingly.

If it is available—say we are willing to cut our income or save in some other area—we have to make a choice. We can postpone or downscale some of the tactics in our plan, or we can decide to spend more on marketing.

Note the first benefit of writing a detailed, reality-based marketing and sales budget. We've put ourselves in position to make a conscious choice, rather than waking up one morning to find we've spent twice as much as we had intended.

It may well be that $60K is too much. But might there be a logical reason for spending six percent of revenue rather than three percent?

"Investment spending"

Suppose we decide to spend the six percent on a 1-time basis, to help launch our firm. Our tactics turn out to be effective. We gross the anticipated $1 million in Year 1, and clear $2 million in Year 2. In Year 3, our growth continues, and we clear $3 million.

In Year 2, we increase our spending on marketing and sales from $60K to $80K, but on a percentage basis that's a decrease from 6% of revenue to 4%. In Year 3, we add a tactic—exhibiting at a trade show—and spend $90K on marketing. But that's a further percentage decrease, to 3% of revenue—the industry standard.

During our first three years we gross a total of $6 million, and we spend a total of $230K on marketing and sales. That's 3.83% of our revenue over the three years. It helps us triple the size of our firm. Was the 6% we committed to marketing and sales in the first year a sound investment? Based on our return, it was a sensational investment.

I used a startup firm as an example of "investment spending" on marketing and sales. A similar scenario could involve an established company that is launching a new product or service.

Don't use your head. Get bids and make projections.

Color Networks sells high speed Internet connection (DSL service) to offices. They developed a tactic. They would put up a kiosk in the lobby of an office building and connect a network in the kiosk to the Internet via DSL. Building tenants would be able to experience the benefits of DSL for themselves on the three computer systems in the kiosk.

When this tactic was first proposed, one line of thought was that it would be too expensive. That was before analyzing the revenue the tactic might produce, and before finding out what it would actually cost.

The target was to sell DSL service to 80% of a building's tenants within 20 days, then move the kiosk and its staff to another building, and so on When we analyzed the cost over a year (about 15 buildings, allowing for friction time) in comparison to the potential revenue, we saw that the tactic had a huge upside. We also realized that the cost of putting in the line was not part of the marketing expense, because that would have to be done anyway to service the new clients. And that the computer systems could be partly written off by using them within the company or selling them when they were no longer needed for the kiosk.

The moral of the story is don't try to calculate the cost-effectiveness of a tactic in your head. Get real bids and compare them to real projections of the revenue the tactic is likely to generate.

Producing ads: the 10% rule

In Chapter 8 I suggested a rule about trade advertising: The cost of producing an ad should be no more than 10% of the cost of placing it. A corollary is that the more you use an ad, the more you can justify spending on it. Please see page 220 for an explanation of the logic of this practical rule, which does not necessarily apply to consumer advertising. I mention the 10% rule again here because it can save you time when you are preparing your budget. Of course, just because the 10% rule is arbitrary and dictatorial does not mean it has to be applied rigidly. Perhaps one year you'll need to spend 15% of the advertising budget to produce some fantastic ads that create a buzz about your products that echoes forever (or at least for another six months).

A giant step forward; now the work begins

With the completion of your marketing and sales budget you will have completed your plan. This is a gigantic step forward for your company, and you are to be congratulated for accomplishing it!

Once the congratulations are over, let's remind ourselves that while writing your plan is a giant step, it is implementing the plan that makes a difference in the real world.

Your plan lays the basis for a year of smart, creative, productive, and cost-effective marketing and sales.

Now the tactics must be implemented, and the plan must be periodically reviewed and updated based on how the tactics are working.

The next two chapters are about implementing and updating your plan.

Make a calendar and budget

Create tactics to market and sell the plan to everybody in your company. To market and sell outside the company, light a fire inside the company.

CHAPTER 10

JUST DO IT!

The title of this chapter amuses me for two reasons. First, I spent many years fighting Nike for market share on behalf of my client, Asics Tiger. Second, in the absence of a rational plan, "Just do it!" can be fatal advice.

But once you've made a plan you're not operating in the dark. Then, Nike's famous slogan communicates an essential truth. Many companies invest time, effort, and money on reports, studies, and plans of all kinds, only to end up with volumes that gather more dust than attention. This weakens a company by wasting resources and building cynicism.

The Dr. Revenue method of creating a marketing and sales plan makes such waste unlikely. By the time the team finishes the planning process they have usually convinced themselves and others to carry out the plan, and often elements of the plan have already inspired action. But nothing and no one should be taken for granted. External pressures constantly act on top management and on marketing and sales people to divert them from the plan.

Don't allow yourself to be diverted! You've made a serious investment in your plan. Now that you've made the best plan you are capable of, "Just do it!" By vigorously pursuing your plan, you'll get results you can use to meaningfully evaluate the plan. As you update your plan, and make new annual plans, your data gets better and your plans get better.

A fight to stick to the plan

We've talked about accounting firm Alder Green & Hasson's decision to hold weekly marketing and sales meetings even in tax season, although the meetings would be shortened during that period from one hour to 15 minutes. It was a battle to write this tactic into the plan, but that was only the beginning of the struggle. Until March 1 of the year in which all this took place, some of the partners did not want to continue holding (or did not want to attend) even the shorter meetings, although they realized the meetings before tax season bore fruit quickly. Nevertheless, they mustered the will to stick to the plan. The meetings helped discover opportunities with existing and new clients into April, May, and June, when many accounting firms slow down. If they had completely halted the meetings it would have created inertia and made it hard to restart, like skipping the health club for three months.

"Just do it!" is not as simple as it sounds. What happens when the first ad or direct-mail package produces a disappointing response, or the new sales incentives don't immediately revolutionize the sales process? It takes discipline to stick with your plan long enough to get meaningful results. Discipline is partly an individual effort of will, but it can be reinforced with organizational and motivational steps, which this chapter describes.

Write your plan quickly

Maintain your momentum! Once your eight meetings are over, the first aspect of "Just do it!" is to guarantee that your plan is promptly committed to paper. "Promptly" here means days, not weeks or months. If you've been following the method described in Chapter 1, this should be easy, because you've been writing and circulating drafts of portions of the plan after each meeting. The only elements you need to add after Meeting 8 are the calendar and the budget, and any revisions to earlier material that result from discussion of the calendar and the budget. Therefore you can finish a draft of the complete plan and put it in the hands of all team members no more than five business days following Meeting 8. Team members should be given two or three days—certainly no more than a week—to comment. Following that, the final draft should be prepared in two or three more days or, at most, another week.

Seeing is believing

I've often had the experience of working on my own marketing and sales plan for two or three months, then finally reading the completed first draft. It's always a revelation. There it is in black and white. Amazing. It's real. I'm confident we can do these things. Of course we can do them. We put them in the plan. We have to do them.

Create belief

Scenario 1: Now that your plan is written, the planning team keeps it secret. Others may suspect that the team has created a breakthrough document, but only the team knows for sure.

Scenario 2: Your team shares the plan throughout the company. Every employee learns that management is committed to implementing this marketing and sales plan over the coming year, and that by pitching in to carry out the plan they can contribute to the success of the company, which will mean more opportunity for everyone.

Question: Which scenario makes it more likely that the plan will be fully and passionately implemented?

Answer: Scenario 2. It's a no-brainer. Once management publicizes the plan, they've made a commitment. They've staked their credibility on carrying it out. Furthermore, those employees who "get it," who grasp the possibilities, will enrich the plan and help implement it. They will see that they can help the company advance and that they can help themselves advance within the company by implementing the plan. Your plan may even include tactics that tie compensation and advancement to carrying out parts of the plan.

Writing the plan quickly maintains the momentum you developed during your meetings. Sharing the plan multiplies the momentum. It contributes to the "Just do it!" spirit.

How about a party or other special occasion to announce and distribute the plan to every employee? You have 500 people? The more the merrier. When everyone understands the positive steps the company intends to take to build business, irresistible power sweeps through your workforce.

What if the competition finds out?

When I suggest sharing the plan widely, some of my clients worry. "What if someone shows our plan to a competitor?" Generally, the benefit of mobilizing your people around the plan outweighs any loss of secrecy. As soon as you carry out your tactics, your competition will know about them anyway. And if competitors discover your plans in advance, they still have to organize to react. What would you do differently if you knew a competitor was planning to launch a particular advertising campaign three months from now? In most cases, little or nothing. (Especially if you couldn't be certain they were really going to do it.) If you did rush into a response, there would be a high potential for costly, poorly conceived tactics.

If your plan contains truly top secret or proprietary information, leave it out of the widely circulated version or include enough to mobilize people around that part of the plan, while excluding details you don't want on the street. Your true secret weapon is circulating the plan widely to generate excitement. Don't distribute the plan to your people routinely, as though it were the new parking policy. Develop tactics to market and sell the plan throughout your company. To market and sell outside the company, light a fire inside the company.

Celebrate the plan with an "all hands" meeting and dinner

In my own marketing, consulting, and advertising company, Professional Marketing Groups, Inc., as we began to develop more formalized planning many years ago, we used the completion of the plan as the focal point for an "all hands" meeting in the evening followed by a company dinner. The meeting was the occasion for giving every person working for the company, including temps and freelancers, a copy of the plan. Not everyone got every number, but everyone got a copy of the plan with our entire strategy and supporting tactics spelled out. I wasn't worried about someone defecting to a competitor or using our plan to steal accounts and go on their own. I felt that it was much more important for the workers and managers to have the real document in enough depth to be able to get into the work and the processes that would be needed to achieve our goals. It worked. We went from approximately $5 million in capitalized billings and $750,000 in gross profit (gross income in the agency business) to over $1.5 million in gross income. The dinner after the meeting was a "fun" time for all with much good humor, but the plans were never far from the table.

Sell the plan beyond your company

Remember "buying is reverse selling." Generate excitement around your plan among prospective employees (see how they react); strategic partners; suppliers; vendors such as ad agencies, design firms, PR firms, and outside writers; and even among key customers. Sharing your plan within your company multiplies momentum; sharing it beyond your company multiplies momentum by an additional factor.

Mobilize marketing and sales forces around the plan

K&M (now a division of Avery Dennison) started out the year with a detailed plan for mass marketing back-to-school items, tax-time items, and an additional promotion between those seasons. At an all-day sales meeting, the plan was introduced in the morning and training conducted in the afternoon. Everything was geared to presentations within a 7-week window to about 150 buyers from Walgreens, Kmart, Wal-Mart, and other chains. Supporting tactics included trade ads, direct mail with coupons, point-of-sale promotions with rebate offers, and other measures that required timely, concerted action. Because all the details had been worked out, with calendar and budget in place, management was able to insure that there was individual ownership of each part of the plan. When problems arose, such as missed delivery deadlines, defective merchandise, or a poorly executed ad, those in charge did not get flustered. They understood the critical nature of their assignments and came up with solutions, not excuses. Sales doubled the first year, and increased 50% in each of the next two years. The planning committee met every month to review progress; its chairperson credited the plan with allowing managers and salespeople to work "on the business, not in the business." Once the complex annual plan became routine, K&M was able to add elements that would previously have been impossible to execute. One year they worked with Warner Records to create a special cassette of 1950s hit songs to use as a premium for launching a new product called "The Hot Ones."

"Just do it!" affects your planning process

Once your company is infected by the "Just do it!" spirit, you will dare to make—and implement—plans that you would previously have rejected as impossible.

It was 1984, and the Olympics were coming to Los Angeles. My firm at the time, The Professional Marketing Group, Inc. (PMG), represented Asics Tiger. We also had as a client Second Sole, an athletic footwear store with a unique selling proposition—buy your shoes from us and get the first re-soling free.

Rick Hertz, president and owner of Second Sole, was a "Just do it!" guy—before Nike developed the slogan. He wanted to open a store in Westwood, near the Olympic Village. He came up with an idea: Asics Tiger should pay the costs of opening the new store. We thought it was an idea that would benefit both of our clients. Our job at PMG was to convince Tiger that they would benefit. This was a complex effort, involving a variety of tactics. I tell the story because it perfectly illustrates how the "Just do it!" attitude can help your company.

Opportunity: We knew that the managers at Tiger corporate headquarters in Japan wanted to fight Nike, Adidas, and others who had set up company stores in the Westwood area. *Goal:* Get Tiger to finance the store. *Problems:* We did not have a lot of time. And why would Tiger need Second Sole, a smallish retailer?

Hunting the Tiger

Second Sole's marketing and sales plan contained an aggressive promotional budget and a reasonable amount of advertising. We thought we could develop a promotion for our nine Southern California stores that would sell a ton of Tiger shoes. The blowout sale would be the first battle in the war to get Tiger to finance the Westwood store. It would focus Tiger's attention on Second Sole.

We created an advertising campaign called "The Great Tiger Hunt." Small ads in several local newspapers announced the hunt. Consumers were told that on certain days during the next two weeks there would be Tiger Hunt pieces placed in the paper. Find all the pieces, paste them on a Tiger Hunt board available at all Second Sole stores, and redeem the completed board for a 50% discount on any pair of Tiger shoes.

Consumers went crazy. One day one of the papers forgot to insert the Tiger Hunt pieces. There were hundreds of calls to the paper and to each of the Second Sole stores. We knew then that we were going to sell a lot of shoes. We sold more Tiger shoes in two weeks than anyone had ever sold in Southern California in two months. Tiger executives were pleased.

After the deep discount and the cost of the Tiger Hunt campaign, Second Sole made only a little money on the high volume sales. But we got attention from Tiger.

Second Sole needed a big dose of the "Just do it!" spirit to launch the Tiger Hunt campaign. We knew we had to do something dramatic to make Tiger sales jump. We recognized that they would jump at the expense of others brands. Nike was our big concern. Day in and day out Nike accounted for over 50% of Second Sole's volume. We could not afford to alienate Nike.

We debated whether we should stage the Tiger Hunt, and decided to do it. Our logic:

- It was a short promotion.

- We could allow Nike to believe that Tiger was behind the campaign. Tiger's marketing agency had developed the idea, and if Tiger financed the Westwood store, they would be paying for it.

- We could promise Nike an aggressive promotion immediately after the Tiger Hunt.

Catching the Tiger

To have the Westwood store open for the Olympics demanded a fast answer. But the Japanese managers were notorious for agonizingly slow analysis of every detail.

We felt that negotiating on our turf would help, so we chose the National Sporting Goods Association show at Anaheim to assemble the Tiger team and sell them on Second Sole's Westwood store. We rented a luxury suite at one of the nearby hotels for the meeting that would decide the War of Westwood. We scheduled this meeting even before we had worked out the content and form of our presentation, because if we had waited, it would have been too late. "Just do it!"

"Explanations tell; shows sell." We hired a designer to render our ideas for the new store. The drawings featured Tiger's striped logo. Tiger would be emphasized, but we would sell other shoes and apparel as well. If the customer could select only a Tiger product, we would not realize the potential sales volume of the Olympic period.

We had built a lot of stores and had a good handle on costs. Our goal was to have Tiger pay most of the expenses of remodeling the store, the rent for at least six months, and to supply the initial inventory at a low price or even free.

Language that sells

We knew that we had to present our points in Japanese, but we did not trust translators to be aggressive enough and focused enough to get an unprecedented fast decision. In previous negotiations, Tiger corporate executives had questioned our translators, and the translators had been more concerned about not offending our guests than about communicating our point of view.

How could we get the Japanese words into the ears of our audience undiluted? The right question leads to the right answer. We prepared Rick Hertz's presentation and then translated it onto tape. At the meeting, Rick would talk for a minute, then we'd run the tape for a minute. We were pretty sure that our aggressive tone and attitude would come through. We were certain that our audience could not question the translator. We could not be sure that our technique would not offend our guests, but we had to go for it.

On the big day we welcomed our Tiger guests, and they settled down for the presentation. The tape seemed to come as a surprise, but the translator's voice was good, the sound system was good, and our audience paid attention.

For the first time, Tiger corporate managers indicated that they understood the importance of an immediate decision. They said, "We need a few minutes to review this among ourselves. Please excuse us. We will be back in less than one hour."

We were on pins and needles. In about 50 minutes the Tiger management team came back, asked a few questions about costs, and said, "We'll do it with Second Sole." We made the sale because our "Just Do It!" attitude was contagious.

Catching the media

No rest for the weary marketeers. We'd sold Tiger; now we had to justify their confidence in Second Sole.

The head of PMG's PR department was a character. Before joining us, he had headed PR for Ringling Brothers Barnum & Bailey. A Hollywood premiere, Klieg lights and all, was only the beginning for the grand opening of the Westwood store. The theme was "Black Tie and Athletic Shoes." Yes, you had to show up in a tux or gown. But it didn't stop there. Jerry's PR team called every reporter that was going to be invited to the opening, and asked for his or her shoe size. Then they sent the left shoe of a pair of brand new Tigers to the reporter, along with the invitation to the store opening. You got the right shoe at the party.

The media turned out in droves and publicized the store. Sales were over the top. Professional Marketing Group had two happy clients.

Your company may not be able to achieve results as quickly as Second Sole's retail operation. Some business-to-business sales take years to complete. No matter. The essential point is the same regardless of the length of your sales cycle. A "Just do it!" attitude leads to bold plans and audacious implementation.

Focus

When it comes to writing your plan, we've stressed the importance of selecting the best opportunities rather than listing so many opportunities that you cannot effectively pursue any of them.

Focus is also critical to implementing your plan.

When you are working on one of the tactics you've selected, work on it. Clear everything else out of your mind and pursue that tactic to the end. Make the extra phone call—or the extra 20 phone calls. Ask the extra question. Check up one more time. Rewrite. Edit. Proofread. Enlist others to proofread. Overkill is better than underkill.

Once you've have decided on three or four good tactics, selecting the best one to work on first is not as important as selecting one and working on it. Hamlet spends five acts agonizing over what to do. In business today you cannot afford that luxury. If you do not have the resources to pursue all your tactics simultaneously, select one and "Just do it!"

Doing more than one thing at a time

This only appears to contradict what I said above about focus. It is a question of how many resources you have. Individuals, even teams, need to focus on the tactic they are responsible for, but with enough competent, self-directed people, you can keep three or four balls in the air at once. To continue to grow once you reach a certain size, you have to learn to juggle. Top management implements tactics it is responsible for, and helps, encourages, and coordinates people who are responsible for other tactics.

Developing staffing in tandem with sales

Affiliated Resource Group, the IBM AS400 computer consulting firm, had $1 million in sales and 14 people on staff. They realized that increasing sales volume and profitability required simultaneously increasing the number of highly qualified, self-directed consultants who could deliver the work and help bring in new clients. Affiliated developed a People Pipeline Project to constantly recruit. One tactic was offering a $100 "interview bonus" to qualified AS400 systems engineers and programmers. Paying a prospective employee $100 just to interview demonstrated Affiliated's aggressive, serious approach and its commitment to not wasting its own time nor that of the interviewee. Another tactic, which we've mentioned before, was Affiliated revolutionary approach of not requiring non-compete agreements. That helped with sales and hiring by appealing to potential clients as well as potential consultants. By adept juggling, the firm was able to open a second office, plan additional offices in other markets, expand advertising and promotion, hire a fulltime marketing director, and allocate more capital to marketing. In just a couple of years, the firm grew to 60 people with $4 million in sales.

Don't bet the ranch

Have you ever noticed that aphorisms come in pairs of opposites? "Opportunity doesn't knock twice," but, "Look before you leap." "Where there's smoke there's fire," but, "You can't judge a book by its cover."

In business as in life, the art is in knowing which advice to apply when. "Just do it!" is as powerful—and one sided—as any other time-tested message. Use your marketing and sales budget to visualize the impact on your business if a tactic fails. Unless you are backed into a corner and you have no alternative, don't "Just do it!" if failure will mean you're out of business. "Just do" something else.

Sometimes, even if you can weather a failure, you or your boss will want a sure thing. More than one client has asked, in reference to a tactic I've recommended, "Can you guarantee that it will work?" I can't guarantee that anything will work. If I could, I'd just pick stocks that would triple and get very rich.

In marketing and sales, there are no guarantees. There are calculated risks, based on measuring cost against estimated return. The calculation may be complex, as in the Great Tiger Hunt, or simple, as in Action Paging's plan to get referrals from existing customers.

Action action

Action Paging is a small company with three stores located in low income areas of Los Angeles. One manager estimates that 80% of his customers are unemployed. This is the bottom end of the market. Nevertheless, sales to existing customers were good and profits per customer were up. But, Action faced a disturbing trend: a decline in the number of customers. Each month, about 10% of their customers failed to renew. It was a battle just to replace them and stay even.

Most of Action's customers came into the stores to pay their monthly bills. To attract additional customers we had a referral policy in place that gave a free month of paging to anyone who referred a new customer.

The program wasn't successful. We evaluated the plan. We did not have the resources to give away anything else. The answer was "Just do it!" Pursue the promotion harder and more dramatically with our existing customers.

We realized we were not taking sufficient advantage of the in-store bill paying. We had every employee wear a "FREE PAGING!" button, and festooned the stores with "FREE PAGING!" balloons and posters. We did not stop at creating an atmosphere that encouraged customers to ask how they could get "FREE PAGING!" To make sure we'd convert as many customers as possible to referral sources, we instituted training. We got all store personnel together to role play the "bill paying" situation.

This just happened as we finished *Profit Rx.* I don't know what the results will be. There are no guarantees. But it's a sound calculated risk.

What if some people "Just don't do it"?

Having a clear plan is wonderful. And scary. It's scary because there is something in writing against which results can be judged. In some of my Dr. Revenue Marketing & Sales Clinics, the result is a look in the mirror for owners and senior managers. Sometimes it becomes clear at the Clinic, as it may during your eight marketing and sales planning meetings, that some individuals are not performing. Or it may become clear later, when they are responsible for carrying out a tactic and they just don't do it. Of course, we have to draw a distinction between a tactic that doesn't work as expected and one that could have been carried out but wasn't.

Many companies have a tendency to carry people who have stopped contributing, or who never did. The result of a good hard look is that some people who have not been performing are reassigned to positions where they can contribute or are cut loose within 30-60 days of completing the plan. This may be painful, but it is part of business life. Companies that succeed find and reward people who can and will carry out their plans, and shed people who can't, won't, or insist on getting in the way.

The real test

I sincerely congratulate you for finishing your plan. Your plan is a giant step in developing your business.

Implementing your plan is the payoff for all your hard work. Sure, it's more hard work. That's why they call it "going to work." But carrying out your plan is infinitely more rewarding—and more fun—than writing your plan. By writing a plan, you have created a method to learn a great deal in a short time. The plan is your design to mold a new reality. But, "Reality is richer than theory." When you carry out your tactics, you inevitably discover unexpected opportunities to take advantage of and unexpected problems to deal with. That leads to updating your plan so it gets better and better, and more and more in accord with reality. That's the subject of the next chapter.

Just do it!

Updating keeps the plan in the forefront of company consciousness. A dog-eared plan is a good plan!

CHAPTER 11

UPDATE YOUR PLAN

You're three months into implementing your plan. There have been no surprises from competitors nor any other unanticipated changes in your market. Your sales forecasts have all proven correct. Each of your tactics has produced its expected result—no more, no less. Every entry on your marketing and sales calendar has been fulfilled to the day, and every expense in your marketing and sales budget has proven accurate to the penny.

Is this a dream or a fantasy?

Yes.

Reality is richer than theory. In real life, especially in an arena filled with variables, such as business, no plan works out precisely as intended.

You wrote the plan to mold reality in favor of your company, and that certainly is the plan's primary purpose. When you started implementing your plan, you became eligible for an extra dividend. By working in an organized way to change your business and your marketplace, you learn more about your business and your marketplace. You can learn a lot from studying; you can learn even more from carrying out tactics designed to produce measurable results.

Say you send out a test mailing of a direct mail piece. The results are disappointing. You call up some of the people who bought and some who didn't. You discover that many of the buyers fastened onto a feature-benefit pair that was buried on page three, and that many of those who didn't buy read your main headline differently than you had intended. Many also reported that they couldn't identify with the drawing showing the product in use. You now rewrite the mailer, making the page-3 point the main one, or at least giving it more prominence, and correcting the ambiguity conveyed in the previous headline. You also kill the drawing and substitute a photo of the product in use. (By the way, if the direct mail piece had produced the intended response or greater, it still would have been smart to call people and find out why.)

The change in the direct mail piece is an update of your plan. It was an update on the fly. The potential for it was built into the plan when you decided to do a test mailing.

In addition to on-the-fly updates of this sort, your team should meet at least every quarter to review the plan as a whole and make any necessary adjustments. The plan is for a year, but a year is just too long to wait for a comprehensive review. In high-tech and other industries where a state of flux is the norm, consider meeting every month or six weeks.

Update when...

...you encounter unexpected problems

CPA firm refuses to dump tactic

Alder Green & Hasson, a Los Angeles CPA firm with a concentration in the waste management industry had an important tactic in its plan: a survey of waste management companies, to be conducted in concert with a trade association. The association unexpectedly decided that its liability would be too great and dropped the survey. The accounting firm considered abandoning the

idea, then realized it had an opportunity to take ownership of the survey and use it as a major marketing tool
instead of, as originally conceived, a PR device. The
accountants realized they had no capability for doing a
survey. Even this problem was turned into its opposite.
By hiring an outside firm they added to the credibility of
the data, while still maintaining ownership of it. Six
years later, the biannual survey is regarded as a major
tool for everyone in the waste management industry,
and has opened the door for the firm to acquire several
important clients. Publication of articles about data from
the survey and one-on-one meetings with clients and
potential clients to go over the data are now critical
parts of the firm's annual marketing plans.

In the example above, when the trade association dropped out the
CPA firm first thought they would have to give up on their tactic. Then
they discovered another way to pursue it, which worked even better.

Sometimes abandonment is the correct response to an unexpected obstacle. The real point is to alter or drop a tactic—perhaps
switching to the next one on your list—but not to abandon the plan.
I call it "bending, not breaking," like palm trees in a high wind.
"Bending, not breaking" is a more likely outcome if the team holds
an update session and calmly thinks things through than if events are
left to take their "natural" (translation: planless) course.

Say you lose a major customer. It happens. Continue along on
cruise control and the damage could be severe. But if the team meets
and deals with the problem of reduced revenue and excess capacity,
maybe you can turn adversity into an opportunity. You might quickly
kill a business-as-usual ad campaign and launch a special two-for-the-
price-of-one introductory offer to pull in new customers fast.

The most difficult problems are often internal. Say your plan
includes a great new promotional program developed by marketing.
You introduce the program to your sales force in Region 1. Similar meetings are scheduled for Regions 2-5. Problem: the Region-1 sales force
actively hates the new plan. They say it's too complicated and they

won't be able to sell it to their customers. You run the plan by a few key salespeople in the other regions. They hate it too. Oops. Update!

...your marketplace changes

Every plan contains assumptions, even if they are unstated. Sometimes there's a dramatic change from the vision of reality implicit in those assumptions. These changes can create new problems—and new opportunities.

Examples:

- You sell electric socks, and the winter in your region is much warmer than anyone had anticipated.

- An overseas competitor introduces a product that has an additional feature and costs less.

- Your biggest competitor goes bankrupt.

- Forty percent of your sales were to Thailand and South Korea, and the Asian Crisis happens.

...the figures come in

You created a marketing and sales budget, and made it as reality-based as possible. Now, the actual bills for advertising, promotion, trade shows—whatever tactics you are pursuing—start to come in. The director of marketing or the sales manager needs to maintain a cash budget. A simple spread sheet is fine. Every cash expenditure that goes against the approved budget needs to be logged and compared to what was budgeted.

Lo and behold, there are discrepancies. Maybe something costs less than expected. It must happen to someone somewhere. More typically, there are overruns. An additional ten to twenty percent over what was estimated for an individual item is not uncommon. Say your company is preparing a brochure to support the introduction of a new product line. You end up paying rush charges because manufacturing is late getting samples to the photographer, or the CEO takes an extra week to approve the copy, or any of a hundred other reasons. Each of these cost overruns must be noted. If the overall budget is to be maintained, adjustments may have to be made in the plans for the rest of the year.

...opportunity knocks

One salesperson has been working hard to get the new product into a major end user through a key distributor. She succeeds! Now it's time to "reinforce success." The breakthrough opens up new opportunities, which the team must evaluate and, where appropriate, plan to exploit immediately, not next year. Examples:

- Now that this new customer is using the product, it may be more attractive to others in the same industry or region.

- The new customer might agree to endorse your product by appearing in your ads or to partnering with you in some way.

- The additional revenue may enable you to pursue tactics you previously put on hold for lack of resources.

The team should also evaluate and plan to solve problems connected with the new opportunity. For example, it will be impossible to fill the new customer's orders and your established customers' order with the present system of production. Who said marketing and sales was just marketing and sales?

...sales forecasts change

To write your plan, you fought to get reality-based sales forecasts from your salespeople. That was probably a major internal breakthrough. Now you have to keep fighting for updated forecasts quarter by quarter. (After a year or two, it becomes a habit and the fight becomes easier to win.) As the forecasts are updated, however, they are likely to differ from the original forecasts. These differences have to be evaluated, and may require modification of your plan.

Should we change the plan?

What do you do when you encounter adversity? A tactic does not produce the expected results. If it just needs more time to work, "stay the course." If it's basically sound but needs fine tuning, tweak it. If it's proven itself a loser, scrap it. But how do you know which is the case? Often, you can't be certain: there are too many variables. Do the best you can based on your collective knowledge and experience, and remind yourself that a reasonable decision is usually better than no decision. There is an art to deciding when to stick with a tactic and when to abandon it. We've all heard the saying, "If at first you don't succeed, try and try again." W.C. Fields modified it as follows: "If at first you don't succeed, try and try again. Then give up. Don't make a damn fool of yourself."

Hidden benefits of periodic updates

The obvious benefit of updating each quarter (or more frequently) is improvement to your plan. There are at least four less apparent benefits:

1) To update your plan requires you to get updated sales forecasts. When salespeople develop the habit of making quarterly sales forecasts, they have taken an important step toward becoming self-managed sales professionals.

2) To prepare for the update meeting, the team members have to reread and the plan and discuss its implementation with other staff members, strategic partners, and vendors. This keeps the plan in the forefront of company consciousness. As one consultant used to say, "A dog-eared plan is a good plan!"

3) If top management is not part of the marketing and sales planning team, part of the update process should be a written report to top management on how the plan is being implemented and what improvements you intend to make. This practice has many benefits, including continued selling of the

plan to top management and keeping everyone on the same page, which minimizes rude surprises for owners, CEOs, and marketing and sales executives.

4) Your quarterly updates are practice runs for writing next year's plan. Once you've done your first plan, every plan after that is an update. The better your team get at the evaluation/improvement that goes into the update process, the better your future plans will be.

Good luck

By putting in the time and effort to write your marketing and sales plan, and by working to carry it out, you have created the conditions for success. Your plan gives you a huge advantage over 80 or 90 percent of your competitors. We wish you good luck. Luck never hurts. By having a plan and working a plan, over a period of time you are likely to benefit from more than your share of good luck, because you have put yourself in position to minimize the bad breaks and take full advantage of the good ones. You already know planners are smart. Here's one additional thought: "Planners are lucky."

Updates of *Profit Rx*

This chapter completes the description of how to write, implement, and update your marketing and sales plan.

As you write and carry out your marketing and sales plan, you will discover new questions, new angles, new variations on the themes. I'd like to make your discoveries available to the readers of *Profit Rx* on a continuing basis. You can send them to me by going to www.ProfitRx.com and clicking on "Contact Dr. Revenue." We'll post the comments that are most generally useful, of course attributing them to you and your company if you wish. Log onto www.ProfitRx.com for these comments, and for periodic updates from Dr. Revenue.

Profit Rx

As good marketers, we deliver more than we promise, so there is an additional chapter, a bonus called "Pulse Report: Numbers to run your business by." Developing and using a "pulse report" is a powerful tool to put you in control of your business. And it adds power to your marketing and sales plan.

Update your plan

Successful owners and managers can give you current, detailed information about their businesses —and they don't have to look up the numbers.

CHAPTER 12

PULSE REPORT

Y ou have a doctor monitor your pulse rate, temperature, blood pressure, and other vital signs to help you decide what steps to take to maintain your health or cure a disorder. Your business, like your body, has vital signs. They reveal whether the company is growing or declining, and they help determine what must be done to continue (or accelerate) growth or reverse decline.

I often ask entrepreneurs, "How's business?" "Pretty good," is the most frequent answer, especially in periods when the economy is perking along. ("Terrible," is a strong second.) Fearlessly, I press on: "How are you doing compared to last month, or to the same month last year?" "Pretty good," they'll say again, often followed by an anecdote about a customer. If it's just that the owner or manager wants to keep his cards close to his vest, fine. But many business people simply do not have the key information at their fingertips. At any time of the day or night, a smart entrepreneur should be able to respond in depth and in detail to "How's business?" I've observed that entrepreneurs who know their numbers tend to succeed over the long haul. Successful owners and managers can give you information like the following—and they don't have to look it up:

- New orders are up 15%

- Shipments are up 20% year-to-date, up 25% last month

- Our receivables are at 40 days

- Our cash is up 10% from the beginning of the year

- Our labor costs are down 15% from January 1

- Our on-time shipping percentage for the past 4 weeks is 97%

Some of the key variables differ from industry to industry and even from company to company. Each entrepreneur should put together a set of figures that reveal the inner workings of his or her business. Of greatest importance are numbers that serve as early warning signs. Why wait for a heart attack when you can take preventive action based on an EKG and a cholesterol level?

An empty seat is lost forever

In the summers I worked on the assembly line of the family business, Haskell of Pittsburgh. My uncle, who was in charge of manufacturing, required that managers report production numbers every hour. His theory was that no production below capacity could ever be made up. To him, the line was like an airplane—an empty seat is lost forever.

Some of our managers disagreed. They felt that hourly counts were ridiculous. They particularly disliked the way my uncle used the counts to hassle them to meet or exceed their quotas.

I have to confess that I sympathized with the line mangers. Nevertheless, the concept that certain numbers were "vital signs" in business was firmly implanted in my mind from those summers on the production line.

Over the years I've learned to look for the numbers which are critical to my business and to my clients' businesses. Today, every business needs to think of the numbers that make a difference. The numbers, positive or negative, that can show the need for action. I call the critical set of figures for a business its "pulse report." When you put together a toolbox to help your company survive and prosper, your marketing and sales plan is your most important tool. Your pulse report is another powerful tool in its own right—and it multiplies the power of your plan. It helps you keep close track of what's working and what isn't. Therefore you can take advantage of opportunities and solve problems that, without the pulse report, would not be apparent until too late.

Elements of a pulse report

Cash

In the Fast Trac program for entrepreneurs at USC we like to say, "Happiness is positive cash flow." Nothing is more important than cash. Regardless of the size of your business, when you have plenty of cash you feel good and when you don't, you don't. Even when you have cash but you foresee a tight situation, your mood changes. It's like being out on a glorious sunny day and suddenly a dark thundercloud appears on the horizon. No matter how well I'm doing, when I'm low on cash I feel nervous, scared, and pressured. My letter carrier can kill a good day faster than just about anybody or anything else. All he has to do is deliver a pile of bills and no checks. Cash is king.

I don't want to make it sound overly psychological, although psychology is important in business. Cash is the fuel your business runs on. Sure, you can borrow money, and debt may be a rational part of your business plan. But ultimately, you have to generate cash to pay your bills, including debt payments. Innumerable businesses have had great ideas, great people, and great products—and have gone under because they ran out of money before all the greatness jelled. To succeed, you must keep a sharp eye on your cash flow, and take whatever steps are necessary to keep it positive.

Accounts receivable

The next best thing to cash is customers who have received your products or services and who owe you money. Strange as it may seem, some companies are better at timely delivery of their product or service than at sending an invoice. Service providers are among the worst offenders in this regard. Until you send an invoice, the account receivable does not exist. Start the clock immediately by generating an invoice simultaneously with delivering your service.

You should always stay on top of two aspects of your accounts receivable:

1. The sum of all unpaid invoices.
2. The time it takes to get paid.

Receivables do not age well. Unless you have negotiated other terms, a receivable over 30 days old is beginning to develop an odor; over 60 days it stinks; and after 90 days it smells worse than rotten fish. Collecting money is the entrepreneur's second most important task. The first is selling to people who will pay in a timely fashion. The problem is that we cannot always know who is in that category and from a marketing and sales point of view it's necessary to take a prudent degree of risk.

Billing potential

Knowing what you can bill and collect during the next 30-60-90 days is another vital sign. Start by tracking orders or projects you are about to complete. Force yourself to be objective. If an order is likely to be delayed for four weeks, don't include it in next week's billing potential. In a service business, let's say you've landed a $100,000 project. The terms call for $20,000 up front and four progress payments of $20,000 each. You've received the first $20,000. Now the trick is to be sure that at each and every step of the way, the customer will see clearly that the agreed upon progress has been made, so that there will be no hold on your money. This may require close communication with the key contact person at the client's company as well as with their accounts payable department. Do not assume that just because you have delivered the next step of the job, and sent an invoice, you will automatically get paid. Their agenda is not your agenda. Accounts payable may wait for authorization from the end user of your services, and the end user may wait for accounts payable to request authorization. All very convenient for the cash flow of your client, but not conducive to your company's health.

Pipeline

Cash is money you have received for completed work. Accounts receivable is money you are owed for completed work. Billing potential is money that you will be owed for orders once they are completed. These are relatively easy numbers to track, because they are based on orders that have been filled or at least started. To ensure the adequacy of future cash flow, there's a vital sign that's more difficult to track, but equally important: business that is likely to come in during the next 30-60-90 days, or whatever the most logical period is for your company.

Reality-based sales forecasting, which we discussed in Chapter 3, is critical to estimating future business. Study the steps in your sales process, and the probability of a sale developing from each step. For example, if you submit 10 proposals, how many do you normally close? One? Three? Five? Seven? You may need to go into greater detail. Salesperson A may close three out of ten, while salesperson B typically closes five out of ten. By constantly monitoring what is in the pipeline—and where it is—you can detect problems in time to act on them. When you are booking more business than you expect, the company must respond by increasing productive capacity, adding people, or finding new resources (or even by negotiating delivery dates). When business is heading down, management must recognize the trend and promptly develop marketing and sales tactics to reverse it. At the same time, management must act to trim overhead so that the reduced gross profit is not dissipated. Monitoring the pipeline heads off crises in production and in cash flow.

Assign value to position in the pipeline

I was in the building in Endicott, NY where Tom Watson, Sr. founded IBM. The team was developing the marketing and sales plan for a hot new IBM product. They had made a number of contacts with companies that were interested, and they were adding up the value of the anticipated contracts: $10 million here, $20 million there—as if they were all going to come through. Suddenly reality interceded. The value assigned to a potential sale was recalculated based on its position in the pipeline. If a customer said yes, I'd like a proposal, maybe that was "worth" 20% of the sale price. If the customer wanted to meet to discuss the proposal, 40%. Additional percentages were added for tryouts, meetings with senior executives, and so on. Even when a contract was drawn up and a deposit received, that was still worth only 90%. It wasn't 100% until the deal was done and paid for.

Beat yesterday

Retailers always want to know "What are the figures for today?" or "What's the number?" which refers to how much we have to sell today to make the forecasted figure or how much we have to sell to be ahead of the same day last year. In many other businesses this is a good way to judge how we are doing. So knowing where revenue is on a month-to-date (mtd) or year-to-date (ytd) basis can be a valuable addition to your pulse report.

Inventory

In manufacturing and distribution businesses the owner's money is on the shelf. Knowing the value of inventory at all times is critical to knowing the health of the business. And once you are tracking inventory, you can take steps to reduce it, or increase it in areas where you are experiencing shortages. Inventory can be spread out all over a plant or even all over the world. It is important to develop quick and dirty systems for estimating inventory, sometimes called "horseback" methods because they could be used while riding by. For example, if the stack is four feet high, there are 1,000 pieces. Or, if I put our brochures on a postage scale, 20 brochures equals one pound.

A watched number is an improved number

The window treatment industry is labor intensive. Therefore direct labor as a percentage of the actual price of shipped merchandise is a key figure in determining the profitability of a company or of any particular product or product line. Warren Shade developed a pulse report that focused on this figure, production line by production line, day by day. Knowing these numbers led to action on production elements that had never previously been managed. Longer runs on certain products reduced the number of times the plant had to tool up. Just setting standards for labor let employees know that management was watching; units were produced in a significantly reduced amount of time. Production of certain items was dropped because it could not be made sufficiently profitable and customers could be satisfied from alternative sources.

Warren Shade also decided to track inventory on a weekly basis, and to set aggressive goals for inventory reduction. The resulting improvement in cash flow enabled the company to reduce its dependence on borrowed money, which lowered the cost of production and added to profits.

Purchases

You want your inventory to be as low as possible without interfering with production or causing missed delivery dates. And you want to know what the cash demands on your company are going to be 30, 60, and 90 (or more) days out. For these reasons, current and projected purchases should be part of your pulse report. Inventory and purchases should be studied together. The purchasing figures should be broken down in a way that makes the most sense for your company: raw materials, parts, outside contractors, shipping. Only by looking at these numbers on a weekly basis can management learn to judge the level of purchases as they relate to the level of production.

Accounts payable

Your pulse report should include your accounts payable, which is just another way of saying it should include purchases you've already taken delivery on but haven't paid for yet. If cash is king, it makes sense to hold off on paying accounts receivable. Within limits. Do not assume that your accounts payable department is carefully evaluating when to pay which bills. Use the pulse report to get a handle on this. Some vendors offer attractive discounts for speedy payment—discounts that may be higher than the interest you could earn by holding the money. In addition to the discount, prompt payment may earn you goodwill (which can be critical when you need help in an emergency) and an excellent credit reference.

Not all accounts payable are created equal. If you buy freight car loads of PVC and pay in 60 days, or even 90 days, there may not be a living individual who even knows, let alone cares. Your salesperson is happy to keep getting the orders and the commissions. As long as you don't exceed the parameters of the accounts receivable system at the PVC supplier, everything is fine.

Take the same approach to an invoice from a consultant who works solo or has a small firm, and you are likely to lose far more than the tiny amount of interest you'll earn by delaying payment. Most creative people and other professionals have nothing to sell but their time, and if they have to spend time chasing after their fee, they resent it. As one copy writer puts it, "I have to come up with hundreds, even thousands of words under intense deadline pressure. Hours, sometimes even minutes, count. Why should it take my client three months to scrawl two words—his signature—on a check?" Pay good professionals promptly and they are far more likely to be there for you when you need them.

Head count
Payroll is generally the largest or second largest continuing obligation of a business. A smart owner or manager recognizes that head count must be carefully controlled. It is easy for a supervisor or department head to think he or she needs another person, or to delay hiring when it really is necessary. Strict rules regarding hiring are critical. To know if the rules are effective, make headcount part of your pulse report and check it on a weekly basis.

OT (overtime)

With some exceptions, overtime is a disease that can have serious, even fatal, effects on your business. Allow liberal use of overtime and you can prove the validity of one of Parkinson's Laws: "Work expands so as to fill the time available for its completion." OT immediately cuts into gross profit. Assume that direct labor is 25% of selling price and materials are 50%, leaving a 25% gross profit. Now assume that the labor content of the job is supposed to be six hours. If the work is done on overtime, at time-and-a-half, that's like paying for nine hours of labor, not six. Now labor will be 37.5% of the selling price, leaving a gross profit of only 12.5%—a loss of half the gross profit. By including overtime in the pulse report—and watching it on a daily basis if necessary—management can prevent Parkinson's Law from bleeding the company dry.

I said there were exceptions. In some industries, overtime is a normal part of the budget. It's used to avoid the expenses related to additional workers, such as fringe benefits, hiring costs, and, in some cases, additional machinery or equipment. In other industries, development or release deadlines require incredible amounts of hours to be worked, in some cases by salaried employees eligible for overtime.

Even in these exceptional situations, the only way to be sure that overtime is fulfilling its purpose, and not being used beyond its purpose, is to track it in your pulse report.

Product mix

If you make or sell only one product or service, you won't need this category in your pulse report. Otherwise, it's important to go beyond the totals and know what is selling, so that you can evaluate the impact of changes in sales on production capability and profitability. All products do not take the same amount of time or labor to produce. All products are not at the same stage of their life cycle. If a product that has been a cash cow for your company is now on its last legs, how is it being replaced in the mix? If a new product is catching on fast, what can be done to reinforce its success? Watching the mix is critical to anticipating the need to reassign labor, reduce or increase inventory commitments, and, with a dying product, to gradually phase out costs such as custom packaging, catalogs, brochures, and operating instructions. Orders for these items tend to perpetuate themselves unless someone is paying attention. Stay on top of your product mix by analyzing it at least monthly, and it will reveal problems and opportunities to you.

Other pulse report items

Customize a pulse report to fit your company. Over the years, refine it with more and more useful numbers and relationships. Most of the items described above will be part of every company's pulse report. Here are some other categories that might apply to yours:

Freight costs and claims

Are we paying too much for inbound and outbound freight? How much trouble are we having with our shippers and why? (For a referral to a great freight consultant who gets paid by the carrier, send email to drrevenue@ProfitRx.com.)

Phone calls or emails to our customer service

What level do we expect? What level are we experiencing?

Walk-in traffic

A vital number for most retail businesses.

Closing ratio

In retail, this ratio measures walk-ins vs. closes. If you submit proposals to potential customers, it measures proposals vs. contracts. Or it could measure sales calls vs. sales.

Telephone traffic in response to ads

A vital measure of activity created by your company's advertising. It's important to track which ad in which publication or spot produced each response.

Other responses to advertising

Bingo cards, coupons, leads generated from trade shows, and so on. Your company pays cash for advertising—what is the return? Now? Previously? What is the trend?

Planned advertising

How much cash is committed to future advertising? When will those payments be due? If it is not too soon to evaluate, are the commitments justified by the response to your present advertising?

Other marketing and sales cash commitments

What sums are committed to brochures, catalogs, Web sites, and other tools that are significant components (5% or more) of your marketing and sales budgets? When will the payments be due? If it is not too soon to evaluate, are these sums justified by the results you're getting now?

Benefit by watching the numbers

If you've ever jogged, you know that when you are conscious of time vs. distance (minutes per mile) you tend to run faster. To control your weight, you "watch what you eat." The Pulse Report is a management team's way of improving the business by assembling its vital signs in an orderly, consistent manner. When owners and managers read the vital signs regularly they learn to see changes and trends. They "sense" what is going on in their business. Everyone in the company works harder when they know that management is on top of things, which is, after all, an important part of its job. Top management monitors middle management, for the overall benefit of the business.

If your company has a "sort of" pulse report, work on making it more complete and using it more. If your company does not have a pulse report, work together to develop the data that is needed and begin using it weekly. A pulse report will benefit any business, and, as we said earlier, it multiplies the power of your marketing and sales plan.

Dr. Revenue's

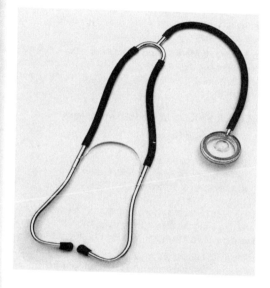

Marketing & Sales

CHECK-UP

BY JOHN S. HASKELL
Professional Marketing Consultant/Professional Speaker

Introduction-*Marshmallow Marketing-The Concept*

- soft sales targets
- undefined goals
- weak market data
- ineffective advertising
- vague promotion schedules

By definition marshmallows are soft, squishy, high in calories, high in fat, and low in nutrition and food value. Marshmallows may be fun to eat, but in business marshmallows must be avoided.

The concept of Marshmallow Marketing provides a manager with a convenient symbol for the soft, squishy, hard to pin down type of thinking that has given marketing and sales a bad image.

Dr. Revenue's Marketing & Sales Check-Up is designed to help you and your staff review your company's marketing and sales plans to ferret out marshmallows and turn these good but fuzzy ideas into hard-edged, building block concepts for immediate implementation.

The Check-Up looks at the following elements:

I.	The Marketing Plan	VI.	Advertising
II.	Market Data	VII.	Merchandising
III.	Definition of Opportunities	VIII.	Promotion
IV.	Development of Sales Goals/Forecasting	IX.	Managing the Plan (Budget)
V.	Identification of Problems	X.	Review System

Within each of these categories questions are posed for you to answer about your marketing and sales plans. If you don't know the answer off the top of your head, find some data, review the facts, and then finalize the Check-Up.

A simple 1-10 rating system is provided for each part. When you have completed the process add up your scores and see where you stand.

The Check-Up is set up for an individual manager. I have found that using this device forces an entrepreneurial professional to deal with the realities of his/her market and recognize the strengths and weaknesses of the company's efforts to create revenue.

Dr. Revenue defines marketing as, "any action or reaction which serves to create (profitable) revenue." Also, "Marketing eliminates excuses by sales people."

Please use the Check-Up as a tool to help your business grow.

Sincerely,

John S. Haskell

John S. Haskell/aka Dr. Revenue
Professional Marketing Consultant
Professional Speaker

1

I. The Marketing Plan

1. Does our company have a written marketing plan? ☐ yes ☐ no
2. Is our plan developed from a series of internal, departmental plans? ☐ yes ☐ no
3a. Do we use outside consulting support to develop this plan? ☐ yes ☐ no
3b. Would a consultant be useful? Vital? ☐ yes ☐ no
4. Is the plan used throughout the year to help guide the marketing and sales process? ☐ yes ☐ no
5. Does our plan contain a detailed schedule of all marketing and sales activities? ☐ yes ☐ no
6. Does our plan contain a detailed budget for all marketing and sales activities? ☐ yes ☐ no
7. Does our company provide for monthly and quarterly monitoring of all marketing and sales expenses versus this budget? ☐ yes ☐ no

Rating on a scale of 1-10 for this section.   1 2 3 4 5 6 7 8 9 10

II. Market Data

1. Do we have good statistical data on our market in general? ☐ yes ☐ no
2. Are the company's sales figures organized to be compared to our market data? ☐ yes ☐ no
3. Do we have some measures of share of market? ☐ yes ☐ no
4. Do we have a fix on competitive volume? ☐ yes ☐ no
5. Do we have a feeling/general idea of each key competitor's overall profitability? ☐ yes ☐ no
6. Do we have (need) a fix on competitions' profitability on key products? ☐ yes ☐ no
7. Do we have statistics on our key customers' volume in specific markets? ☐ yes ☐ no
8. Do we have share of market/growth statistics for each sales territory? ☐ yes ☐ no

Rating on a scale of 1-10 for this section.   1 2 3 4 5 6 7 8 9 10

Rating System: For each of the 10 categories you should rate yourself overall on a 1-10 scale. Review your answers. If over 50% of the answers were "yes" give yourself a 5; if over 80% were "yes" give yourself a 9-10; if less than 50% were "yes" give yourself a 3-0. On page 6 you will find a final evaluation sheet. Put your rating for each section in the appropriate spot and determine your overall score on Dr. Revenue's Marketing & Sales Check-Up.

2

III. Definitions of Opportunities*

1. Do we have any products which have demonstrably superior quality? ☐ yes ☐ no
2. Do we provide any unique services which separate our firm from others providing similar products/services? ☐ yes ☐ no
3. Do we enjoy a reputation, history, or market position that is different/better than others? ☐ yes ☐ no
4. Do we have competencies which are different from competitive firms? ☐ yes ☐ no
5. Is our market growing rapidly? ☐ yes ☐ no
6. Are there products/services we do not presently provide that we could provide to the same customers we now serve? ☐ yes ☐ no
7. Do we have a sales force that is uniquely qualified, or well positioned to sell more? ☐ yes ☐ no
8. Is our company particularly well financed? ☐ yes ☐ no
9. Do we have any vendor/supplier relationships that provide unique, special opportunities for current or new products? ☐ yes ☐ no
10. Do we have new product research and development capabilities that are superior to other firms in our industry? ☐ yes ☐ no
11. Do we have market superiority over our competition in the minds of our customers? Their customers? ☐ yes ☐ no
12. Do we have a superior management team? ☐ yes ☐ no

Rating on a scale of 1-10 for this section.　　1 2 3 4 5 6 7 8 9 10

IV. Sales Goals/Forecasting

1. Do we have quantified sales and profit goals for the current/next year? ☐ yes ☐ no
2. Do we have a sales forecast for any customer who provides 2% of our total volume or more? ☐ yes ☐ no
3. Do we have a sales forecast for all significant products (significant=2% of sales or more)? ☐ yes ☐ no
4. Do we have a sales forecast for all sales personnel who are responsible for customers/geographic areas? ☐ yes ☐ no
5. Were the forecasts in #4 developed by (with the input of) the sales person? ☐ yes ☐ no
6. Are our forecasts updated quarterly? (monthly if needed?) ☐ yes ☐ no
7. Do we have non-revenue goals that are specific? e.g. Acceptance? Awareness? If so, does the company have quantified measures of performance? ☐ yes ☐ no
8. Do we have growth goals that are quantified? e.g. We want to increase sales at a rate of15% annually, or we want to increase specific products' sales at a given percentage rate. ☐ yes ☐ no

Rating on a scale of 1-10 for this section.　　1 2 3 4 5 6 7 8 9 10

*Sometimes the lack of an opportunity points out a problem. Section III and V work together. For every problem there should be an offsetting opportunity.

3

V. Identification of Problems

1. Have we identified specific problems related to the quality of our product/service? ☐ yes ☐ no

2. Have we identified specific problems related to specific types of customers/prospects? ☐ yes ☐ no

3. Have we identified specific problems related to the price of our product/service? ☐ yes ☐ no

4. Have we identified specific problems related to our sales force/sales methods? ☐ yes ☐ no

5. Have we identified specific problems related to the level or range of services we provide to customers? ☐ yes ☐ no

6. Have we identified specific problems related to competitive products/services? ☐ yes ☐ no

Rating on a scale of 1-10 for this section.　1 2 3 4 5 6 7 8 9 10

VI. Advertising

1. Is there an advertising plan for our company? Products? Services? ☐ yes ☐ no

2. Does an outside advertising agency/graphics service that you feel understands the strengths of your marketing and sales programs support the company? ☐ yes ☐ no

3. Does the company get good dollar value for its advertising? ☐ yes ☐ no

4. Is the effectiveness of advertising adequately measured? ☐ yes ☐ no

5. Is the sales force provided complete, effective sales tools? ☐ yes ☐ no

6. Does the company provide complete, effective sales tools to customers (resellers)? ☐ yes ☐ no

7. Do we have a complete, professional public relations and communications program? ☐ yes ☐ no

8. Is there a budget for advertising, public relations, and other activities which is adequate for the company's current needs? ☐ yes ☐ no

Rating on a scale of 1-10 for this section.　1 2 3 4 5 6 7 8 9 10

VII. Merchandising*

1. Do we merchandise our products/programs to our customers? ☐ yes ☐ no

2. Do we provide merchandising assistance to our clients to help them sell our company and our products? ☐ yes ☐ no

3. Do we actively promote our abilities in merchandising to our customers? ☐ yes ☐ no

4. Do we have a written merchandising program? ☐ yes ☐ no

5. Do we have a budget for merchandising? ☐ yes ☐ no

6. Is the budget we have for merchandising adequate to achieve our goals? ☐ yes ☐ no

7. Do we have outside merchandising resources who assist in developing our programs? Do we need additional resources? ☐ yes ☐ no

Rating on a scale of 1-10 for this section.　1 2 3 4 5 6 7 8 9 10

*Merchandising is often hard to understand versus advertising and promotion. Merchandising creates "magic" by using premiums, promotions, point-of-sale displays, shelf-talkers, coupons, contests, etc. with one basic objective—sales motivation. Merchandising strategy focuses on "extra buying incentive" at either the trade or consumer level. Merchandising's net result is an advantage over competition, perhaps by getting a better display, more shelf facings, increased customer advertising support, etc. Merchandising creates excitement.

4

VIII. Public Relations/Promotion

1. Are PR/promotions important to the business? ☐ yes ☐ no
2. Can PR/promotions contribute an incremental increase in profit? ☐ yes ☐ no
3. Do we have a planned PR/promotion calendar? ☐ yes ☐ no
4. Do our sales people know of our promotions well in advance? ☐ yes ☐ no
5. Do our customers know of our promotions well in advance? ☐ yes ☐ no
6. Do our customers consider our promotions of value (profitable) to their business? ☐ yes ☐ no
7. Do our salespeople adequately sell our promotions to our customers? ☐ yes ☐ no
8. Are our promotions more than price promotions? ☐ yes ☐ no
9. Do our promotions impact our overall profitability? ☐ yes ☐ no
10. Do our promotions provide a competitive advantage for our programs/products? For our customers? ☐ yes ☐ no
11. Do we have a plan for participation in trade shows, meetings, conventions, conferences? ☐ yes ☐ no
12. Do we have a specific plan for each show that identifies at least three opportunities and provides a strategy for capitalizing on these opportunities? ☐ yes ☐ no

Rating on a scale of 1-10 for this section.   1 2 3 4 5 6 7 8 9 10

IX. Managing the Plan

1. Do we have a program to implement all phases of the marketing plan? ☐ yes ☐ no
2. Do we have a system in place to assign individual responsibility for each phase of the marketing plan? ☐ yes ☐ no
3. Do we have a budget/control system in place to allow our staff to implement the marketing plan? ☐ yes ☐ no
4. Do we have a milestone chart to monitor the progress of all longer term projects within the marketing plan? ☐ yes ☐ no
5. Do we have company wide acceptance of the marketing plan and understanding of our goals? ☐ yes ☐ no
6. Do we have field sales management that understands the goals by territory? Customer? Product? ☐ yes ☐ no
7. Do we have field sales management that has been trained to work with field sales personnel to implement the sales plan? ☐ yes ☐ no
8. Do we have field sales management whose compensation is tied to achievement of specific sales results? ☐ yes ☐ no
9. Do we have sales personnel whose compensation is tied to achievement of specific sales results? ☐ yes ☐ no
10. Do we have field sales management and field personnel whose compensation has been tied to specific information gathering and specific marketplace activities other than dollar sales? ☐ yes ☐ no

Rating on a scale of 1-10 for this section.   1 2 3 4 5 6 7 8 9 10

5

X. Review System

1. Do we have a system in place to monitor specifics of the marketing plan at all times? ☐ yes ☐ no

2. Do we have detailed reporting systems in place to assess the impact of the marketing efforts on sales? ☐ yes ☐ no

3. Do we have specific reporting systems to relate actual sales to forecasted sales results? ☐ yes ☐ no

4. Do we have systems in place to begin development of new marketing and sales plans as soon as implementation of the current plan is started? ☐ yes ☐ no

5. Do we have a complete understanding of the demands and requirements of the marketing plan? ☐ yes ☐ no

Rating on a scale of 1-10 for this section.　　**1 2 3 4 5 6 7 8 9 10**

Now it's time to see how your company stacks up...

Results

Dr. Revenue's Check-Up Results
You have completed the 10 categories of the **Marketing & Sales Check-Up**. Look over your ratings and list the overall scores for your firm below:

1. Marketing Plan　_____
2. Market Data　_____
3. Opportunities　_____
4. Sales Goals/Forecasting　_____
5. Problem Identification　_____
6. Advertising　_____
7. Merchandising　_____
8. Public Relations/Promotion Programs　_____
9. Managing the Plan　_____
10. Review System　_____

Total Check-Up Score　_____ /100=　_____ %

Market & Sales Improvement Ideas
List below three ideas you have for improving your marketing and sales programs **immediately**.

1. _____

2. _____

3. _____

6

Competitive Matrix

Companies					
your company					

INDEX

Profit Rx

Profit Rx

CONTACT INFORMATION

Profit RX

For questions, comments, additional information, and updates:
www.ProfitRx.com
info@ProfitRx.com
800-332-0258

For discounts on orders of 5 or more: www.ProfitRx.com or
800-332-0258.

Dr. Revenue's Marketing & Sales Clinics, consulting services, and professional speaking

www.drrevenue.com
310-476-3355
800-332-0258
John S. Haskel
1700 Mandeville Canyon Road
Los Angeles, CA 90049-2526
USA

Rick Rhoads & Associates Writing that sells your products and services

www.profitwriter.com
rick@profitwriter.com
310-559-9921
800-55-WRITE (800-559-7483)
3520 Tilden Avenue
Los Angeles, CA 90034-6109
USA